SALES MASTERY: PERFORMANCE DRIVEN SELLING

101 IMMEDIATE Strategies & Techniques to Understanding, Applying, Accelerating & Leveraging the Fundamentals to Selling Success for MASSIVE WINS!™

Sales Mastery - Performance Driven Selling: 101 Immediate Strategies & Techniques to Understanding, Applying, Accelerating & Leveraging the Fundamentals to Selling Success! ™

Dr. Jeffrey Magee, PhD, CBE, CMC, CSP, PDM

Praise for "Sales Mastery"

"Business is all about IT, Jeff's first book on professional selling … Now, Jeff has brought together in SALES MASTERY: Performance Driven Selling a series of strategies and techniques that every Master of Selling would have gladly paid dearly for when they were starting out to have attained greater levels of success faster and been able to build better lasting relationships with their clients from … if you want more, then you need this book!"

* Harvey Mackay … is a nationally syndicated weekly business columnist and author of the #1 New York Times bestseller, "Swim With The Sharks Without Being Eaten Alive!" and "We Got Fired! … And It's The Best Thing That Ever Happened To Us."

"With a bounty of powerfully unique ideas and easy to understand and apply methods for leveraging your own internal assets and working collaboratively with others, Jeff Magee's SALES MASTERY is the ultimate guide for continually moving into higher and higher realms of selling achievement for a lifetime of sustained success. If the key to success is what you're looking for, look no further—this book teaches you strategies and techniques on how to connect with yourself in a way that will unlock your unlimited potential for goal achievement and growth and help you understand how to use your own assets as your personal currency for lasting success."

* Ivan Misner, Ph.D., NY Times Bestselling Author and Founder of BNI®

"Another great contribution to the world of personal and professional development. Jeff details in great clarity what you need to do to reach the top! (this book is a substantial Revision to SALES MASTERY/1.0)"

* Zig Ziglar, was America's motivational, inspirational speaker, and author for nearly 50-Years

"My team and I just finished a full week with Dr. Jeffrey Magee and his mind-blowing program https://www.jeffreymagee.com/performance-driven-selling.cfm.

I can't make it clear enough: After 30 years of being an entrepreneur on three continents and self-proclaimed modern marketer, and after tons of seminars in marketing and selling over these years, I was humbled and stunned by what my team and I learned in just one week with Dr. Jeffrey Magee. Jeff is an absolute master in the art of selling, marketing and teaching excellence in these fields. He propelled myself and my team to a level we didn't even know existed. Jeff is the Gold Standard and his formula and tools are the only ones we rely on.

Our board has just decided to put the whole leadership through Jeff's https://www.jeffreymagee.com/leadership-academy.cfm. We can't wait for him to propel us to the next level."

* Stefan Beiten,, Founder / CEO Argo Ventures Chapter-Chair 2018/2019 YPO Gold Berlin Producer "Planet Earth"

"I have had the pleasure of having Jeff Magee coach and mentor my sales force for over 20 years. The relationship started during my military day, where Dr. Magee's training helped propel my recruiting force into the number one small state in the country.

This relationship has continued beyond, my military days and into my civilian life where on numerous occasions he has tuned up my sales force. Most recently his inspirational pep talks coupled with real world techniques to improve performance aided my Southwest branch finish as the number one BHHS, NV Properties sales force in 2014 and 2015 and in the top 10 of all BHHS branches in the country for 12 consecutive years.

I'm not proclaiming that he can do the same for you, but isn't it worth a meeting to just find out how he's been able to achieve these result time and time again. I respectfully endorse Dr. Magee's teachings, techniques and tools of the trade to any leader looking to not only motivate his team but improve performance.

Feel free to contact me with your questions,

* Aldo M Martinez, Broker/Branch Manager Berkshire Hathaway Home Services, NV Properties

"I took the recommendations of my peers and hired Dr. Magee for two days of training. My sales force team is comprised of national guard recruiters. The training was motivational, but more importantly my team learned new tips, techniques and gained new concepts beyond basic sales fundamentals. Directly after the training, we exceeded our sales/production numbers for over 100 days. Dr. Magee's training works!"

* Randy Higginbotham, LTC, EN, BS, MA, Iowa National Guard

"One of the greatest compliments that I can provide someone is to say that they are a serious student of their specialty and their craft. There are too many who give "book reports" on the material of others -- or who pontificate without qualification. Dr. Jeff is a serious student -- who also possesses a remarkable ability to take what he has learned...and what he is immensely qualified to speak and write upon...and delivers actionable insights to his clients in a compelling manner."

* Scott McKain, CSP/CPAE, Sales and Marketing Hall of Fame

"Jeff is a common-sense guru who goes beyond theory to practical ideas that work to increase revenue and profit. He is insightful, clear and extremely relevant to any organization wanting to compete at an elevated level."

* Roxanne Emmerich, CSP/CPAE, Founder at Institute for Extraordinary Banking

"Dr. Jeff Magee is by far the best performance, sales, leadership coach in business. The intellectual capital this man possess is amazing. The concepts, processes and systems to success will help any company. As a keynote speaker Jeff is the only professional speaker I have seen over 10 times and would attend another 10 events. Make your event or conference a winner and bring in Dr. Magee."

* George Tsafonias, Director of Marketing/Robert Slack LLC/Real Estate

"Talent Development: I had the opportunity to spend 1-1/2 days learning from Dr. Magee at the National Association of Electrical Distributors Sales Management Bootcamp in Austin, TX in April 2017 and also during the 4-hour Strategic Leadership workshop he presented at the NAED LEAD Conference in Denver, CO in July 2017. Dr. Jeff's innovative and rapid-fire delivery of leadership & sales strategies and techniques taught us all many new skills that can be immediately applied in our businesses and will no doubt positively impact our companies and careers for years to come. I have attended many personal and professional development educational conferences and workshops over my 27-year career and Dr Magee is the best of the best. His real-world experience, outstanding educational credentials and expert mastery of his subjects combined with an enthusiastic, engaging delivery style and his passion for guiding others to success makes attending one of his educational sessions feel like you're sitting in a College Masters' Degree Level course."

* Vito DiMaio, Director of Marketing & Employee Development at Stoneway Electric Supply

WOW - More powerful feedback from solo-practitioners, major industry business leaders, military recruiters and sales trainers: * http://performancedrivensellingbootcamp.com/

Sales Mastery

ISBN: 978-0-578-40899-6
US $39.00 CAN $49.00
Copyright 2019 Sales/Business/Marketing//Self
Help/Motivation

Magee, Jeffrey L., Ph.D. CBE, CSP, CMC, PDM
Sales Mastery - Performance Driven Selling: 101 Immediate
Strategies & Techniques to Understanding, Applying,
Accelerating & Leveraging the Fundamentals to Selling
Success! ™

Green, Sheryl, editor
Wittenwiler, Taryn, copy editor
Brandon Wayne, cover design editor
Performance 360 Media Group / Jeffrey Magee, LLC,
publisher

Performance 360 Media Group
Las Vegas, Nevada
www.jeffreymagee.com
406-548-5385
A New Era in Publishing™

For information regarding special discounts for bulk purchases
for business training emersion, large groups, personalized
edition for your group, families and gifts, please contact the
following:

Las Vegas, Nevada
www.JeffreyMagee.com

Table of Contents

Improving Your Communication Effectiveness: The Art of Sending the Correct Signal for Impact

About the Author

Introduction

What this book is not –
A complete and thorough discussion of strategies and techniques on professional selling ….

What this book is –
A powerful fast-track reference guide to professional selling at any level and the accelerated best practices of super achievers.

What this book affords you –
A level of success you could have if you knew you would not fail.

What this book will do for you -
Most selling, recruiting, and client-service professionals' efforts implode in their own minds due to lack of technician and professional abilities. This lack of ability leads to negative internal self-dialogues and sales implosion before even getting in front of the Prospect or client.

What I have learned from every power achiever in selling and from every organization that consistently over-achieves, is that they have mastered:

1. Understanding and deploying Rule 1-52-X™!

2. Understanding, designing, adjusting, leveraging and with focused discipline always adhering to the Work-Product+Frequency Model™!
3. Understanding and deploying Rule 5@5 ™!

As a veteran sales professional, emerging sales associate, business leader or owner, entrepreneur, solo practitioner or sales force manager, your understanding of the fundamentals of selling effectiveness, as well as your grasp of advanced selling strategies and tactics will be directly related to your bottom line.

If you . . .

Close via salesmanship,
Enlist via recruiting,
Influence prescription habits of a physician via detailing,
Solicit new or renewal business via telemarketing,
Or so on, via whatever method you use ... then this book is for you.

This book is about thirty years of selling strategies that work. These strategies are gleaned from my years of experience in many sales venues, including: starting a sales company while in high school, becoming a top Fortune 100 firm sales associate with American Home Products, becoming the youngest certified sales instructor in the world for Dale Carnegie Training, ascending to a vice president of sales position for a national advertising firm, authoring a bestselling sales textbook for McGraw-Hill (published in multiple languages), penning a nationally syndicated weekly sales column, designing the sales training initiatives for the largest volunteer organization in America (the United States Junior Chamber of Commerce), working with the more than 5,000 enlisting recruiters of the ARMY National Guard, Air National Guard, and Air Force Reserve, working with many of the Fortune 100 firms globally for more than three-decades, with highly profitable small-to-medium size companies, Associations and YPO/VISTAGE/CEO2CEO Peer groups!

Best practices have been identified with massive objective analytics for what does and does not work across a myriad of industries. These have been developed through trade research and leading sales force interviewing analytics for predictive analysis in hiring proven personalities for selling success.

In interviews with the masters of selling—Zig Ziglar, Tom Hopkins, Jim Rohn, and Brian Tracy, for example—the power secrets of our time are revealed in detail in this book, along with literally hundreds of other immediately applicable relationship-building approaches for you to benchmark your efforts.

Whether your challenge is to find high-impact quality clients (Customers, members, recruits, or whatever a client is called in your business), or to find ways to grow and cultivate them into champions, this book will accelerate your effectiveness. You will elevate your relationships to the level where clients will generate leads back to you and you will find valuable, immediately applicable solutions within this book.

One of the monthly mental accelerants of the sales professional for the past century has been *Professional Selling Power Magazine*. Every few years you'll find a research-based article that indicates common traits of super successful sales professionals. Having been written by "substantial" individuals, we are tempted to believe that the author is the first to conduct this degree of research. In truth, however, this sort of research has been done time and time again over a period of decades by many of the masters of selling. The beauty is that the research findings usually arrive at some commonalities.

These three key factors lead to increased selling effectiveness:

1. You can increase your selling effectiveness by about 20 percent by recognizing that sales effectiveness is related to SYSTEMS.

2. You can increase your selling effectiveness by about 30 percent by recognizing that sales effectiveness is related to PROCESSES.

3. You can increase your selling effectiveness by about 50 percent by recognizing that sales effectiveness is related to ATTITUDE.

This book addresses each of these three key selling factors. You will find dozens of strategic and tactical maps to greater success. As a sales professional or leader of a sales team, the key selling questions are simple. What have you done lately? What do you do on a regular basis? What immediately needs to be done to increase overall impact and success in selling in the above three areas? Can you specifically point to a tangible act that positively feeds the above three areas? If not, what can be initiated?

Just as one would expect his or her physician, CPA, or attorney to stay mentally sharp and current on trends and technique, we too should hold ourselves—selling professionals—up to the same high benchmark for professionalism and success. I call this process/achievement *SALES MASTERY -*
Performance Driven SELLING: 101+ Strategies & Techniques to Understanding, Applying, Accelerating & Leveraging the Fundamentals to Selling Success. ™ and I use this book to show you how to find, get, keep & grow your business. Consider this your ultimate handbook for selling success.

Section I

Understanding the Fundamentals

Chapter 1

Performance-Driven Selling©
Product IQ = Claims + Features + Benefits + Naildowns: Designing Your Position Statement

Many sales professionals believe that bombarding the consumer with claims of greatness will earn them business. We see this in advertising, sales promotions, and social media, and we hear it from announcers on radio and television all the time.

As you observe your colleagues, notice whether they speak in vague generalities of claims, using phrases like "We are the best" or "We have the biggest, newest, greatest, fastest, cheapest." Phrases containing the "est" words are typically claims, and those same claims could be made by your competition. Salespeople who make "Claims" hope that the consumer will accept those Claims without asking for verification.

Avoid using Claim statements in your presentations, as they can be turn-offs for the consumer. If a Claim is going to be made, then an associated Fact Statement must be offered in the same sentence. For example: "This widget is the best (Claim) in the market right now, because of its X feature (Fact Statement). It has been rated number one in value by *Consumer Reports*, so it offers the quality and reliability (Benefit) you desire."

The Claim ("best") is immediately associated with a specific feature ("X"), which is reinforced by an acknowledged third-party authority (*Consumer Reports*), and the Benefits presented are "quality and reliability."

In many instances, baseless Claims are made by sales professionals who lack the working knowledge of the actual product or service that is necessary to accurately represent an organization. The more working knowledge a sales professional has of all the tangibles or intangibles offered by your organization, the specific facts or features, the better able he will be to point out the Benefits to the consumer.

Master sales professionals have an extensive working knowledge of what they represent, and therefore, of what they have to sell or offer. They have the ability to match up consumer needs with the solutions they offer by describing in detail the facts or features of the products or services they represent. The less working knowledge a sales professional has, the weaker his sales performance will be over time.

In making a simple presentation to a consumer, the sales professional may make a Claim to grab the consumer's attention ("We are the best"), but that Claim must then be immediately associated with an appropriate and corresponding Fact or Feature statement, and with a Benefit statement. It is the Benefit statement that ties the Fact or Feature statement to "What's in it for me?" from the buyer's perspective.

To ensure that the sales professional has correctly connected with what is important to and valued by the consumer, the sales professional finishes the presentation sequence (Product = Claim + Features + Benefit) with a corresponding Naildown statement (a confirming question) that might sound like this:

"And that is the level of quality and reliability that you want, isn't it?"

A Naildown (Product = Claim + Features + Benefit + Naildown) is a positive statement in the form of a confirming question directed toward the consumer to reinforce a key Fact or Feature presented and tie it to the appropriate Benefit.

Getting consumers involved in this process early and showing them how you can partner with them to solve their needs is a fast track to closing sales.

One way to determine whether a sales professional can engage in this most basic dialogue with a consumer is to find out how he responds when asked, "What do you do?" or "What makes your organization better than others?" I refer to the sales professional's response as his Position Statement. In other words, how do you position yourself when given the opportunity to gain another person's attention and interest?

A Position Statement must be very natural, simple, and powerful, so that you tell the other person just enough, but not too much, about who you are. It should be worded in such a way that it almost compels the listener to ask for more information. It should be an automatic response to anyone, anywhere, who asks, "So, what do you do?" Some professionals call this statement an elevator pitch. If you were on an elevator and had only a precious few seconds to answer that question, what would you say that would motivate the other person to get off the elevator with you and ask for more information?

A sales professional's first words create a first impression. Your Position Statement draws upon your basic working knowledge of what you offer: the features, the associated benefits, and how the benefits answer a need expressed by the other person. This is the foundation for selling success.

If I were selling skill-development training sessions to a client, my Position Statement might sound like this:

"I work with individuals who want to significantly increase their ability to interact with others effectively, resulting in better account relationships and more profitable sales."

If someone is serious about wanting to improve his sales effectiveness, he is almost sure to follow-up by asking me more questions. I now have an opportunity to draw upon my basic working knowledge to serve his needs, which results in a sale.

Remember, a Claim is an assertion; a Fact or Feature is a tangible expression of what something does or is; a Benefit is how a Feature helps someone; and a Naildown is a statement that seeks confirmation from the other party that the Claim + Feature + Benefit sequence you have selected is relevant and important to them.

Strong sales professionals have a highly developed working knowledge of what they offer and who they are.

Chapter 2

Performance-Driven Selling©
Why Do I Care? Defining
Your Passion and Personal
Buy-In Factor

The ability of a sales professional (aka recruiter, client services contact, account manager, business development manager, etc.) to believe in what they represent has a direct impact on how others perceive them. When a sales professional buys into what they represent, that has a direct impact on their sales effectiveness. Studies indicate that successful sales agents have a firm "belief" in what they do and what they represent.

Ask yourself a few checking questions right off:

1. What are my values that drive my professional behaviors?
2. What am I passionate about that drives my desire to professionally do what I do?
3. Why did I first come to do this vocation or job?
4. Why did I believe this was important in the beginning to drive me to do what my business card indicates is my position?
5. Do I still believe this?

6. Why should anyone else care or be Interested in what I do or what I represent?

Knowing why you care drives your needs and can help you to deal with the negatives, challenges or derailments that can be associated with sales.

Think about this for a moment: When you believe in something that you do, your passion for it grows. When your passion grows, then your motivation grows. And, when your motivation grows, your buy-in level is likely to become firm with conviction.

Your ability as the sales professional to take care of an existing client significantly increases your sales effectiveness with that Customer. More than any other single factor, telegraphing and sharing your buy-in energy will help you to connect with the Customer.

"Why do I care?" is a question of passion, motivation, and conviction.

As with any serious profession and professional, another way to test your buy-in level of confidence, conviction and professionalism is what you do to continue to push yourself to be the best that you can be. Consider:

1. What was the last educational article I read that elevates my ability to professionally serve my marketplace? Or wrote?
2. What was the last educational book or online post I read that elevates my ability to professionally serve my marketplace? Or wrote?
3. What was the last educational program, class or online learning program I participated in that elevates my ability to professionally serve my marketplace? Or facilitated?

4. Is there a professional certification process related to what I do and am I current?
5. Do I consider myself a Subject-Matter-Expert (SME) at what I do, and how would I validate or prove this?
6. Does my business portfolio represent the results of my being proactive or more responsive to opportunities that come to me?

As a sales professional, you must understand the "why" of what you represent and the "why" of your own buy-in, before you can be expected to represent the organization enthusiastically to the world. It's important to understand your unique buy-in reasons and learn how to share them with the world.

Chapter 3

Performance-Driven Selling©
Identifying the Five Steps of
Selling

Psychologists suggest that in the transaction of selling or buying, whether transactional or relational, five essential steps must be taken by the sales professional because the human brain moves through five essential states when going through the buying/affiliation process. Sales professionals must understand each step, know how to accomplish the sequential objectives of each step, and know how to move the sales dialogue from one step to the next.

The five psychological steps or phases to selling are:
1. Attention
2. Interest
3. Presentation/Solution
4. Desire
5. Close

"Attention" means getting the Prospect's attention despite any distractions or preoccupation. The focus is on breaking their predisposition to get easily distracted as you enter into the next conversational steps. Sales professionals need to identify polite, smooth phrases that can be used to grab a Prospect's attention, establish fast rapport, and move the conversation to the more important second step, Interest.

Think of the Attention step like the awareness phase: how do you grab and keep the other person's attention? You can draw upon a wide scope of ways to do this – words, images, pictures, noises and voices, colors, etc., can be deployed to capture someone's attention so you can move them in the direction you desire.

Once Attention has been attained, your job is to effectively transition into the second step or phase of identifying the needs of the Prospect or Customer: determine whether you can address those needs. In the critical second step or phase, the "Interest" step of the sales process, you must invest ample time exploring the Prospect's or Customer's immediate needs and continual needs and the ways in which you can meet those needs.

The Interest step is the most important step to invest time in. Otherwise referred to as the needs-analysis phase or the discovery phase or the questions-and-answer phase or the identification of the buyer's needs-goals-aspirations phase, this is best accomplished conversationally. Ask thoughtful questions that stimulate informational responses from Prospects or Customers. Take notes while the Prospect is answering, so you can limit the number of interruptions. Some of the best Interest questions are open-ended questions that stimulate dialogue between you and the Prospect or Customer. Asking open-ended questions encourages the Customer to open up and provide you with a quantity of information.

If you analyze your best Customers, you should be able to design a core profile of characteristics of those Customers. From here, you can create a series of qualifying or disqualifying questions as a template that you can use to more efficiently engage suspects, Prospects and existing Customers to further serve them.

Once you have identified the needs of the Prospect via the Interest step, you will be able to determine if they have needs, challenges, problems that you can provide solutions for. If there is no solution you can provide or that you can recommend to them from another vendor, then there is no step or phase three. It is time to shut up and transition out of that conversation. If there is no solution you can offer, any further interaction means you are wasting time talking to someone that can't buy, has no need, and can't advocate on your behalf.

If you do have a solution or solutions, you now have a meaningful engagement need. Determine what is your single most dominant solution and fixate solely on this. So, now it's time to transition into the third step or phase. Make your best Presentation of the appropriate product or service for the Customer. The Presentation is based upon the Claim + Feature + Benefit + Naildown sequence.

1. *Claims* are the assertions one may make in the opening statement, "This XYZ is the newest, best, greatest, fastest" … or any other -est words.

2. *Facts or Features* are the tangible or the fact portion of your statement in regards to what the product will deliver.

3. *Benefits* are the "what this means to the client or Customer" statements and the "what it will do for you." This is the statement or conversational aspect that speaks to the other parties' needs or pain points and will motivate them to want to take action.

4. *Naildowns* are confirming questions you can pose, directly associated to what you have just presented, to solicit immediate feedback from the Prospect, to

33

confirm buy-in into what you have presented ... You want them to mentally take ownership of your presented solution and get them to acknowledge that "yes, this is what I want."

After the Presentation, move the sales conversation toward illustrating how the Prospect or Customer will benefit by proceeding with your recommendation. This fourth step or phase helps to build a level of Desire within the Customer for what you have to offer. Here is where you can present a situationally appropriate story or examples of what their life will be like using your offer.

Of course, a sale is not a sale until the fifth and final stage. Sales professionals must understand how to ask for the order or Close the sales process. This final step in the selling process depends on the ability and confidence of the sales professional. If you are spending undue time on this fifth step, you may not be investing enough time in step two, Interest.

The art of the Close is about gauging the level of receptiveness of the Prospect or Customer. Ask questions that allow you the flexibility either to finalize the order or to digress, if necessary. Focus on two types of closing questions:

1. *Trial Closes* or Alternate-of-Choice are opinion-asking questions. They help you to determine the Customer's readiness to make a buying decision. An example of a Trial Close is: "If you were to go with this style widget, would you want to place the order on account or pay cash?"

2. The *Order Close* seeks a commitment from the Prospect or Customer. This Close question is used when you are confident that the Prospect or Customer is ready to take ownership of your product or service. An example of an Order Close is: "How many of these would like today? To proceed, we need to sit down and start completing an application/contract?"

Every sales transaction involves all five selling steps. The sales professional must be able to gauge how much time to invest in each step before moving to the next step.

Chapter 4

Performance-Driven Selling©
Building Your Sales Presentation
Around the Five Steps of Selling

Psychologists suggest that there are five essential steps to the process or cycle of selling. Whether the selling is done face-to-face, in a group presentation, over the telephone, via email, through direct mail, via the internet or over a social media platform, there are specific objectives for each step in the selling process. We discussed these in the previous chapters.

Depending upon your level of proficiency, you may need to focus more energy on one step or another. And, depending upon the needs of the Prospect or Customer, you may spend more or less time on a specific step in the selling cycle.

Remember Five Essential Steps to the Psychology of Selling:
1. Attention (initial engagement)
2. Interest (needs analysis via controlled questioning)
3. Presentation (illustrating a viable solution to their needs)
4. Desire (demonstrating how the solution meets their needs and illustrating the gains to be attained)
5. Close (gaining the buy-in, whether transactional or relational, of the other party)

If your sales conversation with the Prospect or Customer is effective, you will know when and how to interject an appropriate solution to the Prospect or Customer. Remember, always present to the most dominant and pressing need you have discovered in step two. The elements that a complete Presentation includes, whether about a Product or Service Recommendation, are:

1. *Claim* is the attention-grabbing assertion statement; typically includes some sort of "est" words – "This is the best option for you ..." or "This is the newest ..."

2. *Feature or Fact* statement is the tangible of the offer ...

3. *Benefit* statement is "What this means to you ...." Or "How this will benefit you..." \

4. The *Naildown is a confirming question* to solicit firm agreement or ownership by the Prospect after you have sequenced the previous three elements into a sentence. You now say something like, "And you do want to have ...., don't you?"

As a sales professional, guard against the tendency to invest too much time talking or visiting at step one, rather than establishing good rapport for a smooth transition to the second step. This is where you will identify the Prospect's or Customer's needs and level of interest in what you have to offer. It is important to accomplish step one quickly and move into step two, because with effective questioning in step two, you will find out how much or how little information to provide in step three.

Build powerful Claim + Feature + Benefit + Naildown statements into your response in step three. Become adept at effectively communicating the gains the Customer will realize by accepting your offer. Many sales professionals fail to accomplish this valuable step; but building the want (or Desire) in the mind of the Prospect or Customer works to seal the Customer's mental acceptance of your offer.

If you follow the sequence of the five steps to selling, you will successfully Close and gain the business.

Chapter 5

Performance-Driven Selling©
Attitude's Impact Upon Sales
Performance

In 1910, Professor William James of Harvard University first recognized scientifically that for all of the differences among human beings, we each maintain 100 percent control over one factor in our lives: our minds. Many denounced what he reported and many disliked the label affixed to it. In the 1940s and 1950s, another American psychological giant, B.F. Skinner, conducted additional studies to determine whether James's findings were accurate; Skinner verified the earlier results. Again, others refuted the findings, based on a dislike of either the two individuals or their studies. Ironically, the opposition actually validated the findings. Today, the torch is carried by Dr. Albert Ellis and Dr. Martin Seligman.

With nearly 100 years of scientific research and data, it is amazing that so many people still challenge the findings.

What were the findings? What distinguishes humans from other living beings is that we each have the ability to control our own minds, and our minds dictate our behavior. Another way of saying it is:

"Attitude is ... the internal voices in our head; it is how we talk to ourselves, which influences how we will either respond (logic based) or react (emotion based)."

Or, more analytically, *"Attitude is ... the mental regulator that allows the Neocortex and Limbic System the ability to talk with one another."*

As reported in *"Professional Selling Power"* magazine, a staple among professional salespeople for decades, reports that a sales professional can increase his selling proficiency 100 percent by:

1. Having a **selling system** that works, which can increase sales effectiveness and net results by as much as 30 percent.

2. Following a **selling program or process,** which can increase selling effectiveness and net results by as much as 20 percent.

3. Maintaining a **positive mind-set or attitude,** which has an impact on your perspective and personality, and can influence your selling effectiveness and net results by as much as 50 percent.

As a sales professional, you can increase your effectiveness and bottom-line results by removing all barriers, people, challenges, and self-defeating internal dialogues that are negative and creating an atmosphere that is more conducive for positive behaviors.

Think about this: can you recognize how you feel emotionally and intellectually after a great sale? How do you feel when you are appreciated by others? How do you tend to act in those situations?

How you mentally see yourself or a situation sets off a series of internal dialogues. These dialogues stimulate you to act or react as you do. Look at this phenomenon further: Consider how you get to work each day, who you interact with at work, and what tasks you work on first and last each day. Psychology refers to each of these as a stimulant. It is the stimulants that you are subjected to that influence your mindset. How you interpret a stimulant influences your thinking, and that, in turn, influences your behavioral response or reaction.

Sales professionals must realize that how they see a situation, outcome, or people influences their interpretation. This interpretation then influences their ability to effectively execute each of the five steps to selling. Studies show that:

Activating Event + Attitude (mind-set or interpretation of event) / Behavioral Response = Outcome

To ensure greater positive outcomes, realize that how you manage the stimulant will influence both your mind-set and the Prospect's or Customer's mind-set.

One powerful way to recognize this is to inventory who you hold in your inner circle of confidence. Master sales professionals can trace their successes to many influencers, and among those are the positive-minded individuals they interact with, both at work and at home.

In the 1940s and 1950s, one of the most powerful sales professionals in America was an insurance salesman named W. Clement Stone, who went on to head a multibillion-dollar firm. Mr. Stone called these positive people influencers his "Mental Board of Directors."

Remember the childhood adage:

Birds of a feather flock together.

A positive attitude can enhance an already successful day and neutralize a poor day. Attitude influences the performance of every sales professional.

Chapter 6

Performance-Driven Selling©
Building & Sustaining Your
Selling IQ as Your Market
Differentiator

The sustained professional is unique from others in their profession and market segmentation merely by how they view themselves and what they commit to do 24/7 throughout their career. Can you speculate on what these unique selling personal features would be?

Among many attributes or undertakings, it is the dedication and commitment to the continued improvement of their craft, whether their organization, employer or Customers demand it or not. It is the professional commitment to ongoing personal and professional development that sets them apart from others.

Sales is like any other craft or profession; one would automatically expect a person to be in tune with all current academic and technical aspects necessary to perform at peak performance. We expect the doctor, attorney, engineer and CPA to expose themselves to continued learning to be best at serving their clients. Why would a sales professional have any less of a commitment to ongoing professional development?

Research into leading account managers of billion-dollar organizations and elder sales professionals (those who have sustained a profitable and rewarding sales career for more than 30 years), all reveal a lifelong commitment to reading, listening, observing and learning.

So, what does your internal voice say when you are invited to participate in a learning or training program? If it is optimistic, you are a winner. If you hear pessimism and reasons to abort, you will find that such an attitude has a direct correlation on your immediate and sustained lack of success.

Building and sustaining your selling IQ for success starts with a personal climate survey and a schedule of commitments at such a level that these action ideas are a norm, a routine, a piece of your mental DNA to greatness. Consider:

1. $_____ How much money do I spend annually on my *Hair/Head* (to create the image that I want to project to the world)?

2. $_____ How much money do I spend annually on my *Face* (to create the image that I want to project to the world)?

3. $_____ How much money do I spend annually on my *Wardrobe* (to create the image that I want to project to the world)?

4. *$_____ Combined annual investment of all three (#1, #2, #3), which are investments one makes to project outwardly to the world who one is; superficial Key Point Indicators (KPIs)? Now, let's get to what really matters in the life of a sustained professional engaged in the art and science of professional selling: business development, account management, recruitment, client relations, etc. ... This next assessment question should be a greater annual financial investment than the previous three combined.*

5. $_____ How much money do I spend annually on my *Head* (all intellectual investments – books, audios, product development learning aids and videos, online learning courses, online learning portals, online learning discussion sites, seminars, self-study, educational conferences and boot-camps, online and hard copy publications/periodicals/blogs/white papers, etc.)?

So, how do you ensure your investment of the mind always exceeds any other investment you can make? Simple.

View what you do as a profession. As if there were a "Certification" for what you do, decide the ongoing expectations and commitments required to be compliant with your "Certification". Then create a schedule for completing the following KPIs:

1. Formal educational course work, as if you were enrolled in a college-level program (textbook format, academic-based learning);
2. Informal self- and professional-development reading or audio program participation;
3. Real-time current reading and learning from established leaders in your craft and industry via online blogs, chat rooms, articles, podcasts, etc.;
4. Online self-study work on the craft of selling;
5. Online self-study work on the technical aspects of your organization, department, deliverables;
6. Online self-study work on your product/service offerings/deliverables:
   a. What is the core product that you sell?
   b. What are the reasons for all other products you sell?
   c. What makes your deliverable better/different/more efficient/more cost effective than any other market options?
   d. What is the core Feature of each deliverable you sell?

    e. What are the associated Benefits of each deliverable you sell?

    f. How comfortable are you with the entire line-up of deliverables you have to sell?

7. Field application of what you do at a proven proficiency level of success;

8. Feedback from clients attesting to your professionalism and effectiveness as a sales professional, and thus, representative of your organization;

9. Feedback from peers attesting to your professionalism and effectiveness as a sales professional, and thus, representative of your organization;

10. Feedback from supervisor attesting to your professionalism and effectiveness as a sales professional, and thus, representative of your organization;

11. Peer-to-Peer networking groups of established, vetted, proven leaders in your field to push you forward;

12. Do you have a Mentor or Performance Coach that can calibrate you towards greater successes with accountability mechanisms;

13. Other:

If you're a selling professional and really want to elevate your selling and presentation skills, consider requesting the opportunity to do a full sales presentation/demo for your supervisor/boss. If you are a business owner/selling supervisor, everyone on your team that is in contact with your marketplace should demo in front of you before they ever go live in your marketplace. Brand consistency and brand integrity should be maintained as a universal, and this experience will quickly reveal the depth of your team's selling, product, and market IQ.

If you need to benchmark your Selling IQ and Behaviors, shadow the top sales professional in your organization for a few days before you go live or as a quarterly self-tune-up opportunity. Just like star athletes train with, work-out with and associate with other stellar superstars, so should sales professionals.

It is the sustained professional who is truly unique from others in their profession and market segment that sets the performance bar for others to aspire towards. It is the sustained professional who is committed to a 24/7 lifestyle of professionalism who succeeds.

Chapter 7

Performance-Driven Selling©
Attention Step: Gaining a
Favorable Start to Your
Professional Selling Presentation

Knowing how to gain a favorable start in the selling cycle is critical for maximizing client-interaction time and increasing sales volume. Sales professionals (aka - Customer service representatives, loan officers, recruiters, relationship managers, etc.) must understand the difference between a "professional visitor" and a "professional salesperson."

The Attention step in selling is analogous to taking time to establish a solid foundation upon which to build a home. However you go about establishing rapport and building a relationship of trust, you are, in essence, gaining the Prospect's or Customer's favorable Attention.

Unfortunately, many sales professionals have not thought much about the power of effective Attention-Getting plays in the overall sales process. Others fall into a routine sales opener that may not always work. The objective of Attention-Getting is the same for emails, letters, presentations, voice mail messages, etc., not just the live face-to-face interaction. Here are eight effective ways to gain immediate, favorable, and undistracted attention:

S: Shocking Statement: Start with a shocking statement that will grab attention.

H: Handshake with Meaning: Shake the other person's hand, solicit his/her name, and repeat it twice before letting go of his/her hand.

O: Offer Something: a gesture, gift, assistance, rebate, coupon, or information that will be valued by the receiver.

C: Compliment: Pay a sincere compliment; it could be something about clothing or accessories, conduct, reputation, accomplishment, or standing in the group.

K: Know People by Name: Use names early and often to establish rapport and make Customers feel comfortable with you.

I: Inquire: Start with a positive question; Introduction, have a VIP facilitate a personal introduction of YOU to the power broker Prospect

N: Needs Analysis: Offer a needs analysis or your observations of a correctable problem.

G: Give a Gift: Offer something of value from your organization as a gesture of welcome.

Another powerful Attention-getting conversational starter is to ask a Question Bearing Upon a Need (known as a QBN). In order to use this technique effectively, you must have working knowledge of what you represent, understand the five selling steps, and know the typical Customer served by the organization and what the usual needs are.

A QBN is a positively framed question that is tied to a statement, which is designed to solicit agreement from the Prospect and continue the sales dialogue. The architecture of a QBN is this:

"If there were a way to _____ [Insert the perceived BENEFIT of the Customer.], would that be of interest to you?

The reason I ask is that _____ [Insert your FEATURE/FACT solution to the perceived need.] Perhaps we can do the same for you. In order to determine if we can, may I ask you a few questions?"

A completed QBN might sound like this:

"If there were a way to increase the effectiveness of your sales team, would that be of interest to you?

"The reason I ask is that we have developed a selling system and training program that has significantly helped thousands of organizations to increase their sales effectiveness and overall profitability. Perhaps we could do the same for you. To determine if we can do so, may I ask you some additional questions?" (The last question takes you directly into step two of the selling process, with the Customer's permission and undivided Attention.)

If properly set up, this Attention-getter can pull the Prospect or Customer into your dialogue quickly and allow you to move to step two of the selling process.

Whether you use a SHOCKING opening statement or a QBN, the objective is to determine whether your Prospect or Customer has an interest in continuing the selling dialogue. Gaining someone's Attention serves as the attraction phase of selling.

Chapter 8

Performance-Driven Selling©
The Interest Step: Capturing
Interest Through Consultative
"Stacking-N-Linking" Questions
for Fast-Forward Selling
& Relationship Building

The difference between an accomplished selling professional and someone struggling can be observed in how the Prospect/Customer is engaged. Professionals pull in Prospects through the art and science of powerful questions, the establishment of a relationship built upon conversational interaction and the determination of the Prospect's/Customer's exact needs and how best to meet those needs.

Many times, you may notice that you rush to the Solution Presentation step of the selling process without thoroughly identifying the potential buyer's needs and capacity to purchase those solutions.

Knowing how to gain the confidence of the Prospect and ask relevant, thoughtful questions and make it appear to be conversational takes work.

Remember, first you must sell yourself, and your integrity, to the Prospect and establish a reason for them to trust you and want to engage with you. Then you can discuss their deeper needs and position yourself to present your potential solutions for their consideration.

The questions that can be utilized to identify the Prospect's/Customer's Interest level in your organization, or the sales professional themselves, should be open-ended in nature to draw out of the Prospect/Customer a high volume of initial information. As the conversation engagement continues, the professional salesperson may begin to tighten up the questions used (transition from open-ended to closed-ended questions) and begin qualifying the information they are receiving to determine how best to meet the Prospect's needs.

As a selling professional you have an arsenal of questions. As you reflect on your business and the specific deliverables you may offer, consider vetting questions that allow you to qualify Prospects, and thus disqualify suspects faster.

Open-ended questions seek to solicit high-volume data and increase conversation participation on the part of the Prospect/Customer. Some of these open-ended questions, which can't be typically answered with a single word, simply follow the 5-W and 1-H formula we were all taught in elementary school:
1. Who
2. What
3. When
4. Where
5. Why
6. How

These same question starters used as open-ended questions can also be used to solicit limited amounts of information by prefacing them. The preface directs the Prospect/Customer to provide precise and specific information. There may at times be a need to follow-up open-ended questions with closed-ended questions to confirm information and get clarification of information.

1. You can also use closed-ended questions that are designed to get targeted information. limited information, and/or clarification to previous information. These are great when a Prospect/Customer may become too talkative. Some of these closed-ended questions and preface statements may sound like: Specifically, who/what/when/where/why/how

2. You can strategically use questions to *probe* for more information, to uncover additional selling opportunities, and to uncover additional needs of the Prospect/Customer. You can *evaluate* the types of questions that may be used to gather valuable information and the *chronology* in which they should be used to gain the greatest amount of information.

Questioning should also match the Prospects'/Customers' interest, knowledge and background level. The sales professional would want to increase the intensity of the questions and word selection with some contacts and loosen up dramatically with others. Remember, it is the purpose of the Interest step of the selling process to determine the specific needs of the Prospect/Customer and then determine if there is a way to meet those needs.

There are only three core questions that must be addressed at this third step in the selling process:

... Adjust these questions to sound most relevant given the context of what you represent ...

Is there a need for what you offer? If not, terminate the sales process.
Is there is a capacity to pay for your offer? If not, terminate.
Is there is a timeline for acquiring what you offer? If not and none are to be set, terminate the sales process.

Through the questions and observations that the sales professional engages in at this step in the selling process, they should be looking for indications of the primary interest level of the potential buyer and indications of potential future interest levels for additional selling opportunities.

Use those words in this questioning or interviewing step of the Prospect/Customer, "Mr./Ms. Prospect/Customer, what are you primarily interested in?"

By asking powerful, thoughtful questions the sales professional will have a meaningful dialogue and a more concise "Presentation" interaction with their Prospect/Customer.

Another powerful way to visualize engaging your Prospects and Customers and to avoid getting distracted is to use the Stacking-and-Linking conversational model. Avoid the rush to talk about YOU without getting to know THEM.

By positioning yourself through consultative questions, you are working to build trust between you and the other person, then you are working to identify the other person or party's needs. Their needs will be Immediate Needs, as well as Intermediate and Long-Term Needs. Your questions should be designed to uncover where the needs are that you can solve and be a partner in solutions.

I was taught many years ago a powerful way to anchor in my head a simple stack of images. One balancing upon the top of the next, and each corresponding to types of questions and information needed to build lasting relationships and a better understanding of another person. Instead of trying to remember a script of questions, the Stacking-and-Linking Model accelerates you forward fast.

Here is how the model could work:

1. Visualize from the ground (bottom) upward (top) a stack of images.

2. Then link to each image the kinds of questions or purposes one should use in meeting a new suspect-Prospect or engaging a Customer at a deeper level.

This allows you to chronologically and sequentially engage another person and gain valuable insights for addressing the other person's immediate and potential long-term needs.

With this Stacking-and-Linking Model, you can create one for any demographic, vertical market, deliverables you represent, or for just about any need you have. You can keep mental control of a conversation with another person by having a mental map to follow. When your conversation strays off subject or purpose, this Stacking-and-Linking Model will serve you well, giving you a reference point to where you last were and where you need to guide the conversation back to.

So here is a conversational Stacking-and-Linking Model for use socially or in meeting another person in a professional setting. Consider this image gram and purposes:

STACK IMAGE
PURPOSES/QUESTIONS

A MAILBOX
Use a firm handshake. Don't let go until you get, hear, and say back their name.

A HOUSE (on top of that image)
Ask about where they live and their family. Look for connection points here.

A Fancy Writing PEN (coming out of that House)
Discuss what they do: position, title, longevity there, etc.

A GOLF CLUB (Coming out of the top of the Pen)
Inquire about what they do for fun, hobbies, etc.

A GOAL POST (balancing atop of that Club)
Now transition to GOAL questions: needs, where they are going in their vocation, etc.

And, now YOU
Now inject how you intersect with them based upon the newly gained insights from these image-triggering informational insights, questions, and conversation

You can take this concept to a more serious business-modeling level, as well, with a planned conversational stack of images, which will prompt you to slowly move the conversation forward by gathering chronologically powerful, informational targets. Here is a Stacking-and-Linking Model that I have used for more than two decades as a universal model that begins with Stacked Images that I then Link to purposes, behaviors and questions.

1. Notice the first images below are all about getting to know the Prospect or Client.
2. Then the images chronologically push me to find out about Needs and Prospect/Client Problems.
3. The last images drive me to explore and discuss Payoff/Solution conversations.

Here is another more planned and deep "business-building relationship" Stacking-and-Linking Model. It starts at the bottom and drives you chronologically and psychologically through a sequence of intelligence-gathering questions. Consider this image-gram and purposes:

STACK IMAGE   **PURPOSES/QUESTIONS**

MONEY =Payoff and presenting a solution
SHOVEL = Dig with more Q&A as appropriate
MEAN DOG = What would it mean to not have that problem?
CHAIR = Get them into the conversational chair
PI = What would you be Primarily Interested in?
GOALPOST, BALL & 3-TAGS = In looking at my solution (ball = feature statement), would you be Primarily Interested in Benefit 1, 2 or 3 (the tags represent 3 associated benefits to your feature statement)?
FROWNING FACE = Frustrations or challenge questions to their status quo
CROSS SWORDS = What's not working questions
ICE CREAM CONE = What do you like most about your present deliverables being received or vendor relationship, etc.?
LONG CIGAR = Longevity questions from insights gained from the DESK
DESK = Questions about their role, title, capacity, background, experience, their background DNA …
DESK = Gain their name, firm handshake, fixate on that before proceeding upward and forward, exchange business cards here for reference while talking …

61

The difference between an accomplished selling professional and someone struggling, can be observed in how the Prospect/Customer is engaged through the art and science of powerful questions designed to pull them together, establish relationship, build a conversational interaction based upon chronological, sequential questions with psychological basis, to determine the Prospect/Customer's exacting needs and how best they can meet those needs.

Chapter 9

Performance-Driven Selling©
Presentation Step: What's it
All About?

By asking powerful, thoughtful questions the sales professional will be able to have a meaningful dialogue and a more concise consultative Presentation interaction with their Prospect/Customer.

It is the responsibility of the sales professional to only present a solution for the primary interest uncovered in the Interest stage of the selling process. Always present to the dominant need uncovered through your consultative questions. Don't over present solutions to the myriad of mini pain points or needs they may reveal. If you overwhelm the other person with solutions, they will actually mentally shut down and say "no" to everything you present. Don't "dump truck" everything you can do for someone at one time. Sequence out your solutions to their needs.

Remember, your responsibility is to ensure that you understand the importance of the Presentation sequence of ingredients, so they all come together for a complete response to a Prospect or Customer's needs:

Product IQ=Claim+Feature (Fact)+Benefit+Naildown

Select from your mental inventory the appropriate product/service that will meet the discovered needs of the Prospect/Customer uncovered in the Interest stage. Once that specific solution is presented, immediately guide that conversational Presentation to flow fluidly containing all of the formula ingredients above:

First, the appropriate selected *Product/Service* is identified as a possible solution to the uncovered needs.

Second, conversationally flow into the *Claim* of why you are suggesting it.

Third, conversationally flow into the naming of that *Feature or Fact* tangible.

Fourth, conversationally flow with a transition statement such as, "*...what this means to you...*" with the *Benefit* statement.

Fifth and finally, conversationally flow into a *Naildown*, which is a confirming question that solicits from the other person an acceptance response ....

Concentrate on how you communicate the solution. You want to communicate in such a way that it compels the listener to want your offer/solution immediately.

Also, sales professionals have a tendency to oversell their solutions. Overpromising (and unfortunately far too often this is connected to under delivering) leads to Prospect/Customer skepticism. While there may be an infinite list of options, bells, whistles and colors available, the Prospect/Customer only wants to hear about the combination that meets their needs. The sales professional must have the self-confidence that their solution will work and the control to limit their remarks.

The Presentation should be physically or verbally presented in such a manner that it yells to the Prospect/Customer, "I have been listening to your needs and here is my customized response to you that speaks only to what you say you need."

Realize that you only want to present the associated Features to a Product/Service that are most appropriate for that Customer. Most Products/Services have many Features and Benefits that can be shared. However, if you share all of them at once, then there are no additional dialogue points (ammunition) to present, should that Prospect/Customer inquire for more information.

A concise Presentation response to a Prospect/Customer could sound like:

"Based upon what we have discussed, there are some ways in which we can meet your needs, let me explain."

"The Widget-Master 2000 is the best option for your consideration, as it features the most recently approved and certified technological innovations, and that means you will have the most advanced and efficient widget in the market today. And, you do want the most advanced efficient technology in your environment, don't you?"

The power of the Presentation statement is that it starts with a Claim (i.e. Best option for your consideration), then ties into a Product solution (i.e. Widget-Master 2000), continues with a Feature (most recent technological innovations) statement, then transitions into a Benefit statement (advanced and efficient), with a confirming Naildown question (you do want the most advanced efficient technology in your environment, don't you?).

As a sales professional, understanding the importance of the complete Presentation process is a skill valued by the Prospect/consumer.

Chapter 10

Performance-Driven Selling©
Desire Step: Building the
Emotional Want and Telling
Your Story

Traditionally, the weakest portion of any selling process is selling to the buyers' emotional needs and then satisfying those needs, and thereby, the buyers' wants If the sales professional spoke to the Prospects'/Customers' desires, then the "want" would be satisfied.

With the Desire addressed and built into the dialogue of the sales process, sales professionals would experience less buying resistance and buyer's remorse. Buyer's remorse can result in returned purchases, apprehension of future purchases and even refusal to consider future offers from the sales professional.

One powerful way to convey to a potential buyer that their needs and wants are being addressed is to speak in terms of how they will benefit by accepting your sales offer. And, to do so, we are moving beyond the Benefit statement contained within the Presentation step of the selling process and sharing a word picture (words that convey a vivid picture) of them using and enjoying the offer.

Desire is fed when the potential buyer is lead down a mental path by the professional salesperson to visualize what their life will be like if they proceed with your offer. The sales professional's ability to convey the emotional factors of a purchase will be dependent upon their level of personal buy-in. This is where you paint a picture via storytelling with them in the storyline benefiting from your offer.

A Desire statement packed with vivid word pictures that solidify the entire sequence of Presentation elements might sound like:

"Mr./Ms. Prospect/Customer, if you proceed with the Widget-Master 2000, here is what you will experience tomorrow. You will come into your office as normal, but now as you look out at everyone's work stations, you will notice that as they boot-up their computers, instead of faces of frustration waiting for their systems to become operational, you will see smiles as with the Widget-Master 2000 the systems will become operational instantly. Instead of colleagues being held up from productivity due to slow systems, with the Widget-Master 2000 you will notice less stress and increased productivity."

And to ensure that the word picture that you have communicated (or verbally painted) is stimulating their Desire to want your offer, you can use a Naildown confirming question as an immediate follow-up. It might sound like:

"Is that the type of picture that you would like to be living in?"

If the sales professional has been coached effectively to know the Prospect's/Customer's needs through engaging questioning at the Interest step and has done an effective job at the Presentation step of the selling process, then the Desire step should be fun and automatic.

In order for the sales professional to do a thorough job presenting an engaging and exciting word picture that stimulates the buyer's want and feeds their Desire for the sales professional's offer, they must: (1) Have a thorough understanding of what products/services they represent; (2) Have engaged the Prospect/Customer effectively at the Attention selling step; (3) Gotten permission from the Prospect/Customer to ask questions and effectively found out precisely what the Interest level is of that person/organization; (4) Done a complete job at presenting a solution to the potential buyer in the Presentation selling step; (5) Personally believe in the Presentation sequence which they have presented; (6) Believe in what they do; (7) Know how to weave words together that allow the listener to see themselves in a word picture "using and benefiting" from the acceptance of the offer.

Some sales professionals become great storytellers and this is a great place for those stories to be interjected. Coach the sales professional to avoid inserting stories in the beginning of the selling process as a means to oversell the Prospect/Customer; as this may many times actually turn people off and result in lost business.

However, stories are great ways to illustrate your key points and enable Prospects/Customers to visualize and experience what it could be like if they did partner with your sales professionals as their solution providers. Many times, this is a place where your more senior sales professionals may excel and where more junior sales professionals could benefit from pairing up with them.

Remember the Disney movie scene with the two deer in "Bambi": The more junior sales professional (the fawn/doe, standing on the side of the babbling brook looking upward across the rolling green meadow to where the older Buck stood looking down on them and eating grass commandingly) may bring renewed energy and vigor to a team, and the veteran (the older Buck) can share his/her knowledge, wisdom and perspectives via colorful stories.

The most powerful word pictures are those that place the listener directly into the future-oriented story in the present tense. Desire is further stimulated by using words that capture the creative imagination of the listener (Prospect/Customer) and stimulate each of the bodily senses: see, hear, taste, touch, smell.

Be your own coach - As a sales trainer/sales manager your role is to be that older deer and coach each sales professional's renewed energies in a controlled systematic direction by helping them to see selling as a science with very exacting steps.

Chapter 11

Performance-Driven Selling©
The Closing Step: Getting
the Commitment and Order

The entire purpose of having a sales professional on a team is to match up Prospects/Customers/market needs with what an organization can provide – you are the solution maker. In making that match and building that relationship, the transaction generates a revenue stream from which people are compensated, products/services/deliverables are made a reality and growth/stability occurs.

The professional sales person who can conversationally and consultatively flow through the first four steps of the selling process, yet fails to get the business, is more of a professional visitor, not a professional salesperson (or recruiter).

…There are a lot of ways to ask for the business, the bottom line is you have to ask. Ask often, ask conversationally and ASK!

In getting the final agreement from the potential buyer and attaining commitment from them to have a healthy transaction with you, that is the purpose of the Closing step of the selling process. In arriving at this point in the sales process, you must realize that of the myriad of closing techniques and options, there are really two basic options at this point in the sales process:

A *Trial Close or Alternate of Choice*
is used to solicit feedback from the person whom you have just made your Presentation to, in order to *seek their opinion* on your offer – you are not soliciting a commitment from them at this point.

Realize that this technique is best used when you feel the potential buyer is receptive to your offer, but you are not 100 percent sure at what buying level (low/medium/high) they are. If there is a belief that the Prospect/Customer may not be ready to finalize the offer and purchase, then a Trial Close or Alternate of Choice is great conversational tool.

A *Trial Close might sound like*:
"If you were to move ahead with this offer,
would you want to take it with you or have it delivered?"

"If you were to join, would you want to proceed with the application process now or wait until the end of the month?

A Trial Close or Alternate of Choice question seeks to gain an opinion from the Prospect/Customer in relation to the Presentation the sales professional has made and their Desire to proceed with the offer. Recognize that if the response appears favorable, move directly to a Close or Order Question. If the response is warm or cold, then the sales professional may need to move back to step two in the sales process, Interest and ask more consultative conversational questions as to the Prospect's/Customer's true needs.

In a favorable conversation with a Prospect/Customer in the *Five Steps to Selling*, you may choose to start at step five: simply ask for the business and Close.

A Close or Order Question asks for or solicits a commitment from the person that you have been spending time courting through the Interest and the Presentation/Desire phases. The downside is that by asking for a commitment when you have misread the Prospect/Customer may result in a resounding "no" response. This is very challenging to build back from.

An Order Question is a powerful Close strategy and is designed to attain an action-oriented commitment from the Prospect/Customer.

A Close-Order Question may sound like:
"How would you like me to process your order?" Or,
"Do you want to take this with you today?" Or,
"How many would you like to have me get for you?" Or,
"Based upon our conversation and your comments, let's get the application process started right now?"

Each of these examples assumes that the Prospect/Customer wants to buy and requests from the listener a commitment.

Other ways of closing the selling process and seeking an order from the Prospect/Customer is by offering Alternate of Choice options as a Close strategy. The strategy here is to give the Prospect/Customer multiple buying options.

An Alternate Of Choice Close may sound like:
"Do you want this in red or green?" Or,
"Would you like a single unit or a case?" Or,
"Do want this on a credit card or to be billed?" Or,
"As we complete the application process, do you have a friend or colleague we should be talking to about joining, as well?"

The art of asking for business from a Prospect/Customer, should be very smooth and conversational. If you believe in your deliverable and understand the other person's immediate, intermediate and long-term needs, and there is a match between what the other person needs and what you have, then it is your responsibility to share that solution opportunity with the other party.

There are three very easy, direct and non-threatening ways to Close the sales process with a Prospect/Customer and get the business.

.

Chapter 12

Performance-Driven Selling©
Fine-tuning Your Sales
Presentation Around the
Five Enhanced Selling Steps

Practice doesn't make for perfection. Perfect practice makes for perfection. And sales professionals can easily fall victim to their own bad habits.

Perfect practices by revisiting the Five Steps of Selling models presented in Chapters 3-11, and the conversation flow model, "Stacking-N-Linking," from Chapter 8.

Sales perfection comes from perfect practice, perfect coaching and perfect reinforcement. As a selling professional, your job is to ensure you have reinforcement mechanisms that allow for perfection to shine through with perfect results.

Use this section as a follow-up and constructive review session of the previous chapters.

Chapter 13

Performance-Driven Selling©
Overcoming the Sales Blahs
& Negative Stereotypes

Maintaining a positive appearance and positive mindset as a sales professional is critical to sustained success. Negative situations and people may be a daily occurrence in the life of a sales professional; however, how one handles them can mean the difference between polished professionalism and self-destruction.

To accelerate personal success, one must have a firm grasp and understanding of two key ideas that will differentiate them from the stereotypical negative salesperson.

First, manage your environment for maximum productivity and positive results each day.
Second, treat the sales profession as a profession and continually commit to professional development activities.

An accountant maintains their mark of professionalism as a CPA by attending classes, reading literature on their craft and participating in self-development endeavors to distinguish them from others as a professional. A doctor or nurse does the same to maintain their license to practice. Each of these professionals maintain minimum Continuing Professional Education

Requirements (CPEs) as accredited legitimacy, so too, should a professional sales person.

As a sales professional, you should be able to identify the activities a successful sales professional participates in on a regular basis to distinguish them from just another salesperson – classes, workshops, seminars, Mini-Seminars, books, audio tapes and CDs that they listen to for skill development. As a sales trainer/sales manager your job is to create environments conducive for such excellence to take place.

Build daily work schedules to include activities at the beginning and end of the day that ensure success and positive mindsets (psychology). Recognize that who you associate with at work and at home have a dramatic influence on who you are, the message we project to others and thus how we are perceived over all.

Recognize your blahs and negative slumps are products of the *LIMITING BELIEFS* that work against you and your trajectory success (read *Your Trajectory Code: How to Change Your Decisions, Actions, and Direction to Become Part of the Top 1% High Achievers* by John Wiley for more accelerated mental tools for greatness). **Watch "On The RED CARPET" YouTube** Video link: https://youtu.be/9xVGtzkxzXU

http://www.barnesandnoble.com/w/your-trajectory-code-jeffrey-magee/1120376074?ean=9781119043232&itm=1&usri=9781119043232.).

Birds of a feather, flock together.
Examine what your flock looks like, where they are headed and determine if, in fact, that is a flock to be associated with. If not, make a course correction today to ensure that you land at the destination you desire.

Chapter 14

Performance-Driven Selling©
Using the Sales-Funnel/Sales
Pipeline to Remain Selling/Recruiting
Healthy

Build a solid base from which to consistently be able to contact, connect and pull-push Prospects into your sales funnel/sales pipeline. The consistent, fluid ability to feed your funnel/pipeline and your ability and discipline to maintain balance in your efforts throughout the critical stages of the funnel/pipeline, is essential to consistent sales/closes.

It is critical, as a professional selling person, to understand that the selling process is like a funnel/pipeline with interrelated steps, some of which will require more time than others. In order for a sale to come out of the bottom, there must be ample qualified Prospects in the funnel to be contacted. In order for there to be qualified Prospects inside the funnel, then suspects must be contacted and directed into that funnel of sales activity.

S U S P E C T S
S U S P E C T S
S U S P E C T S
S U S P E C T S
PROSPECTS

PROSPECTS
PROSPECTS
Applicants
Applicants
Contracts
Contracts
Client
Client
Avatar
Avatar

The downfall of most sales professionals is that they don't maintain a consistent level of activity (personal or virtual) at all levels within the Sales Funnel/Pipeline (*More than six actual performance steps or layers in the selling funnel/pipeline taught on our Performance-Driven Selling™ programs*). Sadly, most view the funnel and work from a feast or famine mentality - undisciplined sales professionals spend a lot of time at one level and then they end up rushing and waiting at the other levels. Recognize that you must spend time each day, week, month on all levels equally – if one expects to make sales calls to Prospects, then there must be a proven vetting process to efficiently move suspects into a poll of qualified people and placed into the funnel to contact.

Also, understanding your math within the funnel/pipeline model is critical to getting into a rhythm of effectiveness in all that you do.

Evaluate the present Customer base to determine how many proposals, contracts or applications you had to process to establish that base. Evaluate how many Prospects had to be followed-up with later and that graduated from suspect. This reverse analysis will reflect how much work and time it took to make that one sale.

For each selling professional, your Magic Number™ comes from your actual work product and your effectiveness at understanding the professional selling process and your deliverables as they interface with your marketplace. How many contacts at the top of the funnel/pipeline does it take to get a Customer out of the bottom?

Again ... How many contacts did it take with any given Customer to finally close the order with them and thus graduate them. Then identify how many suspect contacts did it take to get that one Prospect into the funnel, to further work to convert them into a Customer. The point here is that the funnel will assist in sharpening your skill of recognizing how many suspects it takes a sales professional to contact and qualify as a Prospect, and how many Prospect contacts it takes to close one sale?

Successful sales professionals invest ample time on a regular basis to feed the funnel, work the funnel and take care of the Customers that come out the bottom.

Now, reflect on where you presently find your contacts for each level. Successful sales professionals recognize that their ability to Close a sale is only as good as the Prospects that they contact, and those Prospects are only as good as the pool of suspects and markets of suspects that they can identify and market, advertise, promote and expose their offer to.

Chapter 15

Performance-Driven Selling©
Qualifying Your Profile Customer
– The New 80/20 Rule

Many selling/recruiting professionals work hard every day reaching out to every contact that comes their way. They never realize that while there may appear to be a lot of activity there, in fact there may be little real productivity. One way to focus the activity so that it equals productivity is to study the quality of your present Customers to be able to better identify future Prospects and qualified potential next Customers.

Analyze your present Customers to determine if you, in fact, have a larger percentage of your business coming from a trend of "types" of segmentations. This trend, which most sales professionals have, whether they realize it or not, is referred to as a "Profile." Once a sales professional recognizes that they tend to connect with certain types of Prospects better than others, and that in fact more of their business may be comprised of these specific types of Prospects, then they can focus their immediate energies each day to ensure that all of those like Prospects are being connected with.

Commonly referred to as the "80/20 Rule," it is purported that an Italian landowner and economist recognized one day as he took inventory of the Italian countryside that 80 percent of the land and wealth was held by 20 percent of the people. So, too, is true many times in business: 80 percent of our business is held by 20 percent of our clients, COIs, VIP, and market segments. And the reverse unfortunately is true of many unsuccessful sales professionals. They spend 80 percent of their time with those Customers that constitute only 20 percent of the business.

To accelerate ROI on your endeavors, identify the characteristics of the core Customer base, who are they, where are they and how many more of them are there that are not being contacted.

Examine your present Customer base, analyze the patterns and trends and commonalities among them to determine if, in fact, there are some common ingredients among the pool of Customers. If so, develop these ingredients into a Profile that can serve as a map to finding more future Customers like them – as you know these are already successful users of your organization's products or services.

This Profile is a critical turning point in sustained successful selling, as all future marketing, advertising, promotional and selling efforts can be fine-tuned to speak to these people first. Once you have a profile of characteristics, write them down on a sheet of paper. Now look at each entry one at a time, figure out what questions you need to ask of every next person you meet to determine if they possess these similar profile traits, characteristics, elements.

Now analyze within the Sales Funnel (Chapters 13-14) how many Prospects did you have to contact to graduate each individual Customer? Then analyze how many suspects you had to contact to graduate that Prospect? Now you can tighten that contact loop and become more proficient at contacting and working each contact to shorten that selling process and amount of time invested to make a sale.

Chapter 16

**Performance-Driven Selling©
Avatar - Designing a Qualified
Suspect Profile to get to
Qualified Prospect Profile Faster
for Increased Sales Efficiency
with Everything You Do**

Call it your Avatar, Sales Persona or Prospect Profile, it's all the same. Knowing the traits, characteristics, behaviors, etc. of what constitutes a good lead based upon the reverse analysis of what a *great client looks like* is essential to strategically calibrating your every selling endeavor.

You can have an Avatar for your organization and an Avatar by product, service, or deliverable categories (SKUs).

Great sales professionals never run out of qualified Prospects. That is in part due to the fact that they are consistently putting their name in front of and mining areas where they know there are Qualified Suspects in order to talk business with Qualified Prospects.

Professionals need to examine how they Prospect for leads and where they tend to get such leads. Recognize that **a Qualified Prospect is someone who at a minimum:**

FIRST, has a need for what you offer;

**SECOND, has the capacity to buy/join/want; and
THIRD, has an urgency to do so now.**

With this formula in mind, the sales professionals job is to ask two questions:

1. "What do my Suspects look like?"

2. "How would I detail this description even better if I were attempting to develop a Qualified Suspect Profile

Design a short series of questions that allow you to professionally, respectfully vet a person to determine if they are a Suspect, Prospect or neither ... We have designed a series of ten questions we ask in our business to determine if the person we are engaging is a fit for us or not, and that list of sequential questions has not changed in ten years – it is golden and aligns with every activity we do.

Once you know the question to qualify or disqualify the Suspect to be a Prospect, then you can work to recognize your "Magic Number" – the number of contacts it takes to get from Contact2Contract.

Recognize that it's easy and simple for sales professionals to fall into the trap of waiting for the leads/contacts to come to them, and not many Suspects will do this. However, it takes time to find these Suspects and get them into the "Sales Funnel." Further, it takes more time to work the Prospects in the funnel to get a Customer to fall out of the bottom. Thus, when a sales professional realizes that they have no new leads/Suspects to work, because they have been consumed with the middle or bottom of the funnel, they are now at a point where they need to find and contact new Suspects. You must realize the need for even and consistent work at all three levels of the funnel. In the final analysis, the sale can't take place if you are not continually feeding the funnel with Qualified Suspects.

Successful sales professionals can't be all things to all people. A sales professional must understand what the characteristics are of that ideal candidate that they connect with best and tend to graduate the most of. This well-defined "Qualified Suspect Profile" then guides all future actions (marketing, networking, promotions, advertising, etc.).

Your responsibility is to recognize exactly what a Qualified Suspect looks like and then work to develop a Profile of each. This will assist in differentiating between a potential Suspect to engage in the Five Steps to Selling process in anticipation of that Qualified Suspect becoming a Prospect, and avoid one who might merely be someone looking to talk and waste your time.

With a clearer understanding of your targeted Qualified Suspect Profile in mind, you can examine the contacts they make to determine the level of engagement that is appropriate. As you examine how much time is invested in building the relationships forged at the suspect level and ultimately transitions into the Customer level, you can channel efforts accordingly.

Most sales professionals invest a majority of sales energies where the easiest Suspects/Prospects/Customer -rich environments are. Studies done in the late 1990's by Frank Ruck and Jeff Magee determined that most Customers come from merely 10 percent of available market options.

Known as the *Ruck-Magee Curve*™ (see below) the sales concentration business typically center on the known possible 10 percent. Armed with a better understanding of what a "Qualified Suspect Profile" looks like, sales professionals can invest more time in desired areas and avoid others.

View Suspects to your offer as aligning into a sales curve, the "Ruck-Magee Customer Curve", which indicates that there is always about 10 percent of the suspect pool that can be easily graduated into Customers. There will always be about 10 percent of suspects who will never become a Customer for you. These will also be the forgotten middle 80 percent, which represents potential Customers available from the middle suspect pool.

Sales professionals need to first ensure that they spend time Prospecting with those Suspects that their experience and research indicates typically graduate into Customers. Then invest time where most sales professionals forget to work, in the middle of the suspect pool that calls upon the sales professional exercising diligence. Also, realize that there will also be a percentage of suspects that will *never buy* your offer, so don't waste time with them. These are people that like your competition or don't like your offer, period.

"Ruck-Magee Customer Curve™"

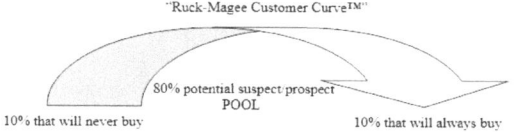

With a clear Qualified Suspect Profile in mind, you will be better able to recognize a contact in the middle of the curve that best matches a solution that you offer. You can accelerate your rate of growth by, then, tapping into the 80% factor that everyone misses. I refer to this segmentation as Market Potential or Market Opportunity. The 10% that will always buy your or a competitor's product is important. However, every lost sales is what most comparisons are drawn from, or what is referred to as your Market Share.

Chapter 17

Performance-Driven Selling©
Overcoming "NO" in the
Sales Process by Understanding
the 3-Step Psychology and
Applying F3

The greatest defeater to selling success is when the sales professional takes a "no" personally. Sales Professionals that succeed, understand that professional salesmanship begins when the "no" enters the conversation. Realize that when someone says "no", they are referring to the offer as they have just heard it, not to the sales professional as a person.

If your questions are confusing, your presentation flow discombobulated, and/or your ideas incoherent, the easiest thing for a confused mind to say is , "NO!"

Every sales professional has heard the statistic: most Prospects become Customers. Thus, the sale takes place after the Nth rejection – you have to know your industry, marketplace, and deliverable to understand how many "nos" to expect and to have fact-based responses at the ready. ***Professional Selling Power*** magazine reported a study done by www.JeffreyMagee.com that indicated most sales take place after at least five rejections.

The important question to know, is at what number "no" do sales professionals typically give up on a Suspect, Prospect or Customer?

Think of "no" as a question in hiding. "No" is merely a verbal response to an offer; then the art and science of selling begins. The questions that a sales professional must then ask are:

1. Does no mean not right now (timing issues)?
2. Does no mean I don't have the money to buy it right now (revenue/budget/ billing issues)?
3. Does no mean I don't have the authority (buying power/decision-making ability)?
4. Does no mean we can't use it or don't need it right now (appropriate need level for that specific offer only)?
5. Does no mean I don't want to make the decision (decision makers are changing and your contact may be leaving and doesn't want to get involved in the offer right now, but maybe their predecessor will desire to do so)?
6. Does no mean I don't recognize a compelling need that I have or a solution you represent?

Determine what they mean by "no" before accepting it as a final answer. Engage the other person in a conversational manner and don't get defensive or be intimidated by their "no." A great way to structure your conversation is to utilize a three-step psychological engagement approach:

1. **FIRST - Qualify** what you have just heard as the objection or no statement. This is easily done by merely restating it in their own words and then asking for confirmation. Never use your own words or appear confrontational, just restate what you heard.

2. **SECOND – Clarify** what you heard by putting it into context based upon fact, logic, and data. You do not want to challenge them, but rather, engage them conversationally and present additional, new information to them to help put your offer into context.

3. **THIRD – Close** that interaction based upon what you do at step two and their response. If they process your new data and are accepting, you would continue with your sales presentation as if they never objected. If they do not accept your new third-party data, politely wrap up your conversation for that day. They are not going to buy and any further interaction at that moment will cause them to passive-aggressively work against you after you leave.

Another way to address the "no" is to use a three-step conversational model called a *Question-Bearing-Upon-A-Need.* Start your response with a preface sentence when you've received a "no" response that you feel may not be legitimate. Something like:

1. *"I can appreciate your concern with (insert what they just said as the "no"). Let me ask you, if we can address this concern fairly would there be any other reason that would hold you back from considering my offer?"*

2. *"The reason I mention this is, (insert a benefit statement that you have delivered to a previous Prospect who recognized your proposition and bought/joined/etc.). Perhaps we can do the same for you. Let me ask you a few questions.*

3. *"May I ask you a few questions?"* And now defer to your consultative-relationship vetting questions.

"Knowing" exactly what "no" means gives the sales professional conversational power in the selling process.

As a new sales professional, recruiter, sales manager and even seasoned professional, pay attention. If you have heard a genuine "no" or "objection" to your offer and professionally addressed it in such a way, that you were able to proceed to a commitment and sale, it will prove valuable in the future. There are really very few original "no" or "objections" that you will encounter the more you engage the marketplace.

The F3 Formula is a classic, professional and effective way to address a "no" or "objection." I have seen it attributed to individuals going back more than a century. When utilized correctly, F3 is a powerful way to eliminate "no" and "objections" and move to more sales closures.

At the time you encounter a "no" or "objection that you have heard before, that past solution becomes the point of your present tense conversation:

1. F = I can appreciate how you FEEL (acknowledger and empathy statement) …

2. F = Others I have worked with FELT the same way upon initially considering my proposal (illuminate that their concern is not unique and that you will address it) …

3. F = What they found was … (provide a solution in second person context to their concern by addressing it, resolving it, dispensing with it and moving back to your selling conversation as if that "no" or "objection" had never been presented) ….

Feel, Felt, Found (F3) is a powerful way to address and resolve "no" and "objections" conversationally when they arise, so you can sell more, sell better and close often.

Chapter 18

Performance-Driven Selling©
Dealing with Objections

Many sales professionals experience fear and anxiety when a Prospect or Customer utters an objection. In order to minimize this fear, train yourself to be aware of potential objections and have logical effective responses at the ready.

Many times, an objection may be a question in disguise. As a sales professional, you must become very adept at listening 'into' the objection to determine what question is not being asked. By making this determination, you can then guide the conversation in a constructive direction. Listen closely, respond (a logic-based response) and don't react (an emotional or defensive response).

When dealing with an objection, you want to engage the other person in a conversation. Utilize the following three-step approach:

1. **FIRST - Qualify** what you have just heard as the objection or no statement. This is easily done by merely restating it in their own words and then asking for confirmation. Never use your own words or appear confrontational, just restate what you heard.

2. **SECOND** – **Clarify** what you heard by putting it into context based upon fact, logic, and data. You do not want to challenge them, but rather, engage them conversationally and present additional, new information to them to help put your offer into context.

3. **THIRD** – **Close** that interaction based upon what you do at step two and their response. If they process your new data and are accepting, you would continue with your sales presentation as if they never objected. If they do not accept your new third-party data, politely wrap up your conversation for that day. They are not going to buy and any further interaction at that moment will cause them to passive-aggressively work against you after you leave.

An objection is simply a response to an offer that we have not personalized enough to show them the value of accepting. Work more diligently on the Interest questioning stage of the sales process and the Presentation solution stage, and the volume of "nos" will decline and the percentage of closing successes will go up.

In order to determine if an objection is the only obstacle to making a potential sale, consider using an **"Objection Qualification Question"** like:

1. "I can appreciate your concern with _____ (insert their exact objection statement here) _____.

2. Let me ask you, if we could address your concern satisfactorily, would you be in a position to move ahead with what we are discussing?"

This question will help in determining whether or not there are further obstacles or future objections that may arise. This sort of question also allows you to determine whether the objection is real or if there is something more substantial that you need to uncover.

By confirming this objection, you can focus on the exact issue. If addressed, then the Presentation phase (the third step in the selling process) can proceed directly to the last step, asking for the Order/Close.

Obviously, after asking the above question, if the Prospect/Customer is reluctant to proceed you may want to ask another probing question:

"Obviously, there is something else causing you to hesitate, would you mind sharing that with me?"

This question works to draw out the hidden, and possibly, the true objection from the other party.

If the objection moves to resistance, ask questions to requalify whether the person meets the criteria developed in *Performance-Driven Selling Chapters 15-17* to determine if, in fact, you have been talking to a Qualified Customer.

As presented in *Chapters 16* and *17*, a "Qualified Prospect" is someone who at a minimum:

1. has a need for what you offer,
2. has the capacity to buy, and
3. has an urgency to do so now.

Understand that once the precise objection has been identified, it is now up to you to determine if that objection can be addressed, and thus, put to bed. If not, you cannot continue the selling process as presented in previous *Performance-Driven Selling* chapters; you must stop and go back to the second step of the Five-Step Sales Process (asking great questions). Then continue to the third step (present the most applicable and powerful "Claim-Fact/Feature-Benefit-Naildown" sequence that you can). See *Performance-Driven Selling Chapters* 3 and 8 for review.

The Naildown question is a powerful way to remove the objection and move back in the conversation to where the objection last came about.

The "Sandwich" technique can help you address objections. To do this, respond to an objection" in three steps (three statements):

1. (visualize the base piece of bun/bread) = positive reference or statement.
2. (visualize the piece of meat/substance) = objection or negative issue.
3. (visualize the top piece of bun/bread) = positive reference or statement.

As the top piece of bread is placed and a corresponding statement given, the Naildown would act as toothpick holding the entire formula "Sandwich" technique together.

Here is an example of how the "Sandwich" technique may sound:

1. *"I can appreciate your concern with ___(insert objection)___ [this first part of the sentence serves as the base bun and is an empathy statement]. That is a genuine concern [this is the meat, substance], there are several ways we can address this [top piece of bun, positive response], _____.*

2. *This does address your initial "Objection," doesn't it [last response is a Naildown]?"*

If you cannot resolve the objection at the present moment, but it may resolve itself over time, save this Prospect as a lead to be contacted in the future when their objection is no longer valid. They may actually be a great future Prospect for cultivation as a Customer.

In this situation, find a polite conversational way to bring your sales discussion to a close; leave; send them a follow-up "Thank You" note,; and maintain their name in your lead-generation file for future review and possible marketing contact purposes.

Section II

Applying the Fundamentals

Chapter 19

Performance-Driven Selling©
Identifying the 4 Core Sub-Decision
Makers to Every Transaction

Recognize that when an individual makes a purchase, there are four different sub-decisions that must successfully be addressed for the transaction to occur. At any one of the four core sub-decision levels a "veto" can take place.

Many sales professionals become so intent on the presentation of the facts/features (what something does) and the benefits (what value it brings to the buyer or how it will serve them), that they corner themselves by not having addressed a core decision factor.

Studies indicate that in every buying and selling transaction, the buyer will always make four minimum mental sub-decisions while evaluating an offer. In some selling presentations, there may be multiple decisions makers involved in the process, each responding to a different mental decision.

The four core mental decisions considered in every buying transaction are:

1. **Financial -** Can we afford it and does it make economic sense? How do the financials work, etc.?

2. **Technical** - Does this offer address what we really need? Does it address our technical requirements, regulations, laws, project needs, personal needs, etc.?

3. **Use** - Will we really use it and gain enough use for the investment/price/cost? Will the person that this is being bought for use it or will this be another source of conflict back at home/work? Does the Prospect even see themselves in your solution using it?

4. **Coach or Advocate** - This is the person or internal voice that likes the offer and may like the sales professional and encourages you to just "go for it". They may serve as a champion of the offer and can be powerful gatekeepers for gaining insight about the other four decision makers and how to engage them.

Be careful, if your entire sales presentation is dependent upon this single sub-decision maker making the deal go through, you may be in trouble. The other three sub-decisions and internal voices may serve to veto your offer when you are not there to defend it.

Sales professionals must recognize that every successful Presentation needs to address all four respectfully. If any are not addressed professionally and the sales transaction takes place anyway, this will only result in future disaster.

1. **Buyer's Remorse:** Occurs when a Customer buys something (or in a recruitment, the Prospect joins an organization based solely on only one sub-decision point), gets home and then realizes that it has caused a financial problem or burden on them. They realize that they are not really using the product or service as intended and they got caught up in the emotion of the sales transaction and did something that now logically

doesn't make sense to them. They may return the item, or if they keep it, they may never return for future business opportunities.

2. **Intimidation:** Occurs when a Customer reflects back on what they purchased and realize it has too many gadgets, too much power for them in respect to what they actually needed, or it's overly technical for them. What seemed easy during the Presentation is now intimidating.

3. **Frustration:** Occurs when a Customer reflects back upon what they bought, realizing that they did not really need it, nor will they really use it, and then recognize that the Coach got the best of them. Now they become mad at themselves and resentful towards the sales professional and organization they represent.

That mis-selling can create future selling challenges and problems. Successful selling centers on, addresses, and does not avoid speaking to those four core mental decisions. In fact, a cornerstone of successful selling involves qualifying your Prospect/Customer to ensure that they can:

1. Afford the offer;
2. That the offer speaks to their specific requirements for performance;
3. That they will, in fact, use and benefit from the offer; and
4. That they are really satisfied with the offer and desire it.

Successful selling addresses four core mental decisions every time.

Chapter 20

Performance-Driven Selling©
Designing Core "Disqualifying"
Questions to Save Presentation
Time and Increase Your Closing
Ratios

The sales professional's ability to conversationally ask the hard questions is critical to sustaining sales success. To accelerate your ability to serve others, learn how to politely and conversationally ask 'disqualifying' questions to vet a Prospect's ability, desire and commitment to entertain your offer on a serious level.

Three of the hard issues sales professionals must feel comfortable discussing are:

1. Financial parameters
2. Use Requirements
3. Timeline constraints

Sales professionals must realize that the solutions to these issues tend to drive most buyers' initial decision-making processes, so they are doing the Prospect/Customer a disservice by avoiding them. Ask simple questions like:

1. "Does this proposal/offer fall within the financial parameters you were expecting?" Or, "Is there a budget range we need to be sensitive to?" Or, "Will this address the financial situation you are in?"

2. "Does this look like something that can be easily used to address your needs?" Or, "What do you like most about what we are talking about and looking at here in respect to __(insert the product/service being discussed)__?" Or, "Can you see yourself doing/buying this and benefiting from it?"

3. "Is there a specific time window that you were looking to have this by?" Or, "Is there an urgency to getting this _____ and having it in use?" Or, "Are you ready to start now?"

Along with the many questions that a sales professional may want to ask a Prospect/Customer, there are always universal question targets that must be addressed. The earlier you ask these questions, the better you will be able to determine how best to meet the Prospect's/Customer's needs. This impacts your progress towards a close or assists in determining if you can't meet the needs of the Prospect, in which case terminating the dialogue may be the best course of action for both parties.

The point of Disqualifying Questions is to assume that every Prospect wants your offer so that you can start qualifying them by eliminating the objections or derailments to the Close, as early in the process as you can.

Chapter 21

Performance-Driven Selling©
Selling to the Five Different Age
Segments in Society Today
with Tailored Approaches:
Motivating the Centurion,
Baby-Boomer, Generation
X-Y, Millennial, and Generation Z

Today's workplace consists of, for the first time in recorded history, a very unique demographic trend: five distinct age segmentations. How each has been raised, conditioned and operates ranges dramatically. The ability of the sales professional to make this recognition and tailor their words, approach, questions and overall presentation to a particular generational segment will significantly impact one's selling ability, and thus, closing ratios.

Census statistics and data charts in _COACHING for IMPACT: Generational Connectedness_ (_by Dr. Jeffrey Magee and Dr. Jay Ferraro_), a managerial leadership text written in 2000, established the trend that we have (and will now always have) in the employment workspace five distinct generational segments. The characteristics, behaviors, belief systems, nuances, and motivational drivers of each may, at times, have similarities and, at other times, vast differences. Understanding these will directly impact your ability to engage and sell to each. Consider:

1. **Centurions** are those workers, (and thus potential buyers) born before 1950. Estimated to be more than 55 million individuals.

2. **Baby-Boomers** are those individuals born between 1950 and 1970. Estimated to be at more than 43 million individuals.

3. **Generation X-Y** are those individuals born between 1970 and 1990. Estimated at more than 30 million individuals.

4. **Generation Millennial** (also known by some as the dot.com babies and the mosaic generation) are those born from 1990 to 1999. Estimated at more than 26 million individuals.

5. **Generation Z** are those born after 2000. Estimated at more than 53 million individuals.

The approach with each generational segment is not a matter of good versus bad or right versus wrong. Rather, how you engage with each needs to directly correlate to the way they were raised and conditioned.

How you engage in dialogue, what you might or might not say, may not always be how you speak and act with your peer group. For effectiveness with a segment significantly older or younger than you, actions may have to differ.

For example, studies indicate the following characteristics of each segment:

1. **Centurions** are more conservative, will scrutinize change, have more loyal behavior patterns, are very

patient, are more formal and structured, like meaning in what they do or commit to, are relationship driven and defend associations, etc. They like one-on-one and face-to-face interactions and printed documents to hold, read and study.

2. **Baby Boomers** are more results oriented, power- and action-focused and tend to be more concerned with image/reputation and materialism. They are conditionally patient, relatively structured and formal in their public impressions and actions, etc. While some may like interactions and communication exchanges like the older Centurions, they may also like some self-directed interaction via the internet.

3. **Generation X-Y** is fast-action oriented, likes net worth options, is centered on "me-ism" and is not very loyal to or patient with long-term commitment needs in the professional world. They tend to resist structure or formalities and feel that everyone is their equal. Some of their decision models are independent of the old rules preferred by Centurions and Baby Boomers and they tend to be more internet connected and social-media driven by established platforms.

4. **Generation Millennials** are into extreme actions and offers, differentiating themselves from the pack, and are not very loyal or patient. Their loyalty is conditional upon their wants; they are not very structured and tend to shy away from formalities, have short interest or attention spans, question authority, want relationships as a source of identity, and are entitlement driven, etc. Their communication exchanges tend be less personal and more internet based, including fast picture/image interactions. They are quick to change opinion based on common social media trends and beliefs; they are more apt to trust too fast and assume what they read is correct; they typically possess a wide breadth of knowledge on lots of differing things, but not a subject-matter-expert

depth of knowledge on any one item. Parents are a major pillar of support in their young adult life and have great influence on their lifestyle choices. Connectivity across a wide range of touchpoints/platforms is smart interactivity with this demographic.

5. **Generation Z** is a more complex generation from their elder Millennials and Generation X-Yers. This demographic is searching for deeper meaning in what they do, want deeper and lasting relationships, like structure, are not easily loyal, but once committed, are very loyal. While they are comfortable and like technology they are apt to choose one-on-one interactions. They typically have short attention spans and like change stimulation, etc. They challenge the need to change for change's sake and want to be more patriotic than some generations before them. Connectivity with this demographic is measured by quality; they prefer a myriad of touchpoints; they like follow-up; and knowing that those they associate will be there for some time ...

The success of the sales professional in engaging each segment is contingent upon their ability to understand these variances.

Chapter 22

Performance-Driven Selling©
Selling to Gender-Specific Needs

Topically, this is a powerful insight to effective strategic and tactical engagement of your marketplace for better engagement and selling effectiveness – this is a market reality and this is not selling gender bias.

Sales professionals have known for decades that the buying styles of men and women have some similarities and some vast differences. The advertising world has studied, tested, and conducted focus groups; ran split campaigns; created different ads, pricing, colors, sizes, names, smells, etc., all in an attempt to determine what works best for men and women. While some very definitive answers have been determined, including a large number of similarities among men and women when in a buying mode, there are still a lot of unknowns.

For your marketplace and deliverables, recognize that how one engages a male versus a female Prospect or Customer may need to differ in respect to their buying behaviors, but not in the level of professionalism afforded to each.

This understanding will greatly influence how you navigate through the Five Psychological Steps to the Selling Process. The gender of the Prospect/Customer may influence how the sales professional engages the other persona and what their need-level drivers may be:

1. Engage in Attention-getting conversations, as a component of Step One of the Five Steps of Selling. Women tend to be (there are exceptions) more relational based and want to feel comfortable with the sales professional before revealing personal information, which is required in Step Two of the selling process – Inquiry/Interest. Whereas men tend to be more aggressive and bottom-line oriented and are quicker to answer or respond to initial questions. Men may also be less engaged in Step One, whereas as a woman may be more engaged. Learn to recognize conversational signals ,as in some situations the gender behavior may actually be reversed.

2. Men may want to be more specific in one single area within the questioning phase of the selling process, Step Two – Inquiry/Interest, whereas a woman may have a wide range of differing questions or answers they want to reveal, all interconnected.

For example, when making decisions around financial matters, men may more often be more oriented towards power, control, and authority in their interactions; while women tend to be more security, safety, and long-term focused in their orientation.

In working with the United States National Guard to determine why men versus women join the military, there are five distinct differences that drive each to their decision. While similar decision drivers are among each's top ten list, the first five are radically different. Knowing this allows you to recalibrate your approach as a selling professional.

3. Men in the Presentation step typically want the bottom-line results that the product/service will generate. They tend to want to focus on the features and benefits that

are of interest to them. Whereas women may also want these tangibles, in the Presentation step they may also be looking for how the product/service correlates to their bigger picture responsibilities in life and how it may be perceived by others.

It is important for sales professionals to recognize that products/services have a wide range of Features/Facts-Benefits. These Features/Facts-Benefit statements may change given a situation. There may be a time when there are certain Features/Facts that will be more effective to share with a female buyer than with a male buyer.

This understanding will guide the wordsmithing you engage in: the examples, references, testimonials, communication touchpoint differences, collateral materials, follow-up engagements, and how you engage one gender versus another. Study gender-specific deliverables, businesses, associations, and affinity groups to benchmark what you do and learn best practices from others that you can incorporate into your style.

Remember, people buy for different reasons. In this book, we have identified several of the influencers to those decisions. Like it or not, one of which is gender.

Chapter 23

Performance-Driven Selling©
Selling to Individuals One-on-One

The annals of recent sales history are full of exceedingly powerful people in the sales world reaching the pinnacle of their industry, all with a similar story. When they engaged in conversation with people, they made that person feel as if they were the only one on the planet to talk to. This may seem a little silly within a professional selling conversation, yet it really is a critical factor of those that are genuine and successful at serving others – connectivity.

1. Mary Kay Ash of Mary Kay Cosmetics fame was known for opening her home to her sales stars at conventions, rewarding super achievers with pictures, handwritten notes, and of course, the pink Cadillac. Many also know, have heard stories about, or personally experienced the opportunity to speak with Mary Kay. She shakes your hand genuinely and firmly, holds onto your hand or arm, looks you directly in the eyes and addresses you by name. She looks at you the entire duration of the dialogue.

It was widely claimed that she never looked beyond you to see if someone more important had entered the area or became distracted with other items around her.

2. Sam Walton of WAL*MART was famous and the stores continue to be successful for many reasons. One is that the stores are manned at the front door by an individual whose sole job is to "Meet and Greet" all arrivals and make them feel like they are home – a smile, a name, a gift or an offer to help.

As a sales professional, realize that any signal sent to a Prospect/Customer that they are, in fact, not as important as someone or something else, can give the Prospect/Customer cause to tune the sales professional out.

... You can take this to the next level when evaluating how giants like AMAZON and Alibaba have simply systematized this same approach using analytics on-line for the same user experience. Great is always great and in essence no one has really revolutionized anything, the rules that work simply evolve and adapt to new realities!

When engaging the Prospect/Customer in one-on-one situations, here are just a few guideposts to help you to avoid all potential distractions and focus fully on the other person. It is critical to:

1. Make eye contact (can you remember the eye color of the last person you talked with?).
2. Notice the color of the hair and hairstyle.
3. Take vivid mental notes or better yet, take physical notes: Use your smartphone to take notes, or exchange numbers in real time so you can create a directory file and add your conversational notes in real time.
4. Call them by their name. Get their name and correct pronunciation. If follow-up correspondence is necessary, get the correct spelling of all names – don't assume spelling.
5. Remember the talk-to-listen ratio should be to listen twice as much as you talk (remember you have one mouth and two ears, utilize them in that ratio).

6. Dialogue to find something that you may have in common with them (geography, hobby, schooling, vocation, industry, etc...).
7. Establish rapport by finding out where the other person sees themself in relationship to using your product or service (defer to the conversational 'Stacking-N-Linking' model taught earlier in this book).
8. Conversationally get the other person to share what their 5W, 1H are in respect to why you are face-to-face with them. Find out what their goals and needs are in this interaction of B2B, B2C, C2C, etc.
9. Take notes and track what their real core needs are on both an immediate level and long-term basis to determine if there is even a legitimate reason for you to be in their presence.

Building a relationship with people one person at a time can be done more effectively if the sales professional first connects with individuals one-on-one. Here is a simple and silly game to see if you really do connect with the other person; or, when you meet people are you so preoccupied with your internal agenda that while they are talking you are not connecting? Consider ...

Chapter 24

Performance-Driven Selling©
Selling to Groups, Using
Rule 80-10-10™

When presenting a product or service solution to groups, the process becomes a more involved activity. With an increased number of decision makers involved in the process, the sales professional must analyze ahead of time the vested interest level or lack of vested interest of each participant in the group.

Most sales professionals in a group-presentation process attempt to engage all participants from a generalized universal approach. This can cause the sales professional to defend positions and statements when challenged by one member of the group. In many instances, the group presentation, which could have been easily managed, becomes unmanageable and may implode.

Sociology studies group dynamics and has found that when a grouping of individuals come together, that group tends to be comprised of three distinct subgroups:

Rule 80/10/10™

1. **80 percent** of the group tends to be neutral on issues and waits to see in which direction energies and momentum goes. Then they channel their commitments in the same direction. Technically, one could label this group as Transmitters or Followers of a norm. These 80 percents or Transmitters/Followers are influenced by one of the influencers or one of the two 10 percent subgroups.

2. **10 percent** of any subgroup tends to be influencers in a forward constructive direction and these are referred to as Transformers, or who are known in selling as your Allies, Centers-of-Influence, Advocates .... They tend to transform a norm into greater yield.

3. **10 percent** of any subgroup has the potentiality of being detractors, defeaters, complainers, negative, challengers of anything that challenges their comfort zone or fiefdom. These are what I call the Terrorists. They have the potential to interfere with the group presentation and the possibility of any acquisition.

Selling to groups can be difficult because the sales professional is merely one percent of the group dynamics. Without the pre-work of an ally, champion, advocate or Center-of-Influence buying into your proposal, it becomes easy for the Terrorist to position themselves and appear more powerful than you and thus attract Followers to their side of the interaction.

In most group presentations, sales professionals can fine themselves investing a disproportionate amount of time with Terrorists at the expense of forward momentum. The primary reason for this is that when the sales professional engages the group, they are one little percent, engaging 100 percent of the group. This makes sales professionals easy prey for the larger and seemingly more powerful 10 percent of Terrorists.

Remember, the Transmitters/Followers channel their energies in the direction of the most formidable influencer subgroup. However, Transformers are not dumb. They will not share their views if they feel the environment is not safe or if they sense that the majority wants to go in another direction.

Before any group sales presentation, ask yourself which individuals have the capacity to fall into which subgroup when you engage them. More importantly, ask yourself if you have any Transformers lined up behind your impending proposal. If not, reconsider the timing of your group interaction. A sales professional can always gain support for their ideas and offers by engaging potential Transformers before the group engagement and getting buy-in from them. You can connect with them one-on-one in advance via email or telephone or just huddle with them immediately before you walk into your presentation.

These individuals can be strategically used in your sales presentation to gain support and buy-in from the Transmitters and to silence the Terrorists – remember Terrorists are not dumb, so they won't challenge you if you have a support network. Transmitters will always align themselves behind whichever force tends to talk first, fastest and loudest.

There are two ways in which you can analyze a group to determine which individuals have the greatest likelihood of being a Transformer for and to you. These Transformers serve as strategic stakeholders in you and your offer. You can recruit a Transformer in one of two ways:

1. **Identify individuals who you have a connection with** - that you like, get along with, are your friends, who like you, or who may owe you a favor.

2. **Identify individuals who have the most to gain by your offer -** based upon their positions, title, rank, age,

sex, race, tenure with the organization, etc.. Look for individuals who may have a vested interest level in your offer and approach them from that perspective.

By approaching targeted Transformers prior to a group engagement and getting their buy-in (you may have to be flexible enough to make some adjustments to the offer to gain the Transformers' buy-in), the sales professional now enters the group interaction with a support network. And the leverage here is that the Transmitters/Followers will align themselves behind your pre-arranged Transformer. You, thereby, gain additional momentum, buy-in and increased individual (B2C) selling opportunities by better engaging the group (B2B) more effectively and conversationally, with less defensive posturing.

The sales professional might start off by saying something like:

"I would like to talk to you all about XYZ Product/Service. I have had the opportunity to visit with Susan, Tom and Roger and they feel this is a great idea, so let me present the proposal and get feedback from the group ..."

By strategically name dropping the people that you have garnered support from, you draw in the Transmitters while not having to put any one person on the spot. Be careful not to mention a name and pause as if to invite a supportive comment from them, as putting them on the spot can backfire.

Selling to groups demands that the sales professional be comfortable with the Five-Step Selling Process and engaging each member of the group as a whole more strategically.

Chapter 25

Performance-Driven Selling©
Selling to Culturally Diverse Needs

In a world of political correctness and hypersensitivity to others, it is still a matter of fact that many sales presentations are sabotaged by the sales professional's inability to make cultural adjustments while presenting. It is critical that you realize the "do's" and "don'ts" when engaging those who may be of different cultural backgrounds.

Years ago, I worked with one of today's leading diversity experts, Ms. Lenora Billings-Harris (*see www.ProfessionalPerformanceMagazine.com for regular diversity performance articles*). We recognized that there are four critical ways to gain a better understanding of diversity issues and how to market sales to those segments. Consider:

1. **Knowledge** – learn their ways and especially their language. The language will direct you to what that segmentation holds important.

2. **Understanding** – read books, watch videos, hang out where they hang out to learn their ways, values, beliefs and what they associate value to.

3. **Acceptance** – accept them on the terms in which they want to be accepted. The Golden Rule doesn't apply in diversity matters; as how you may want to be accepted may be in violation of something that is held sacred to them.

4. **Behavior** – match your behavior to theirs.

As a sales professional it is critical to focus on diversity to enhance one's ability to connect and sell more effectively.

Working with and selling to culturally diverse groups mandates that the words, mannerisms, nonverbal communications signals, materials used and how the relationship is managed, be altered with respect to the ethnicity being engaged.

Once you are able to affect this connectivity, cultural connections can actually accelerate your selling effectiveness and closing ratios. You can even assimilate others to your deliverables once they see a strategic benefit. And this is a critical piece of your homework as a sales professional, identify the 'what's in it for me' (WIIFM as Zig Ziglar made so famous) point for the recipient and present accordingly.

Chapter 26

Performance-Driven Selling© Differentiating Your Offer/Approach via Unique "Selling" Feature Number One

Differentiating your offer by the tangibles offered is a hallmark trait of veteran successful sales professionals. Marketing has found that an organization or person can differentiate themself in a marketplace by examining their Unique "Selling" Features (USF) aka Unique Selling Proposition. This is the first of two USFs to be examined in our series.

USF #1 identifies all of the specific factors (tangibles and intangibles) that you offer and that your competition does not.

In essence, the USF #1 is centering in on all of the things you offer: the "what" factors. Many times in the marketplace, a Prospect/Customer may have a really difficult time seeing the true differentiators, or the "what" of your offer, as being genuinely different than what others offer. At this point in the Prospect's or existing Customer's mindset, your offer may blend into the sea of options being presented to them. Instead of standing out as the choice among options and offers, you are blending in as if your USF is truly not unique.

While USF #1 (remember Unique 'Selling' Feature) is about four core variables in the consumer's mind. What you have/do that is:

1. *Better* than **what** they have now or is available in the marketplace, or
2. *Faster* than **what** they have now or is available in the marketplace, or
3. *Different* than **what** they have now or is available in the marketplace, or
4. *More Cost Effective* than **what** they have now or is available in the marketplace.

Sales professionals must recognize the importance of being able to have a depth of knowledge on all of the unique things that they represent (in respect to the product or service they represent). Knowing all of the unique "what" factors allows the sales professional to have an informed, educated and conversational engagement with Prospects/Customers. And this is why it is critical to have comprehensive knowledge of your deliverables.

It is from a thorough understanding of the Customer's or Prospect's needs, which is the art and science of the needs analysis and interviewing phase, to be able to get the other person (B2B, B2C, C2C) to reveal their needs and match those to solutions you possess.

If a sales professional has limited knowledge of the totality of their "what" factors, then they will miss many selling opportunities. Once the USF #1 is presented, it serves to grab the other person's attention. However, you must associate the corresponding Benefit of a presented USF. It is the Benefits that motivate a person to become a buyer; facts alone do not compel a person to want to purchase with you.

For example, Burger King has differentiated itself for years in advertisements by using USF #1 when it says:

"Our burgers are flame broiled."
This statement differentiates them in the sea of fast-food hamburger options by communicating to the Prospects/Customers in their marketplace that if they want a unique hamburger, they need to visit Burger King, (Our USF is better for you and different from other traditional fried market offerings).

As a sales professional, it is critical to know, and your responsibility to know on a macro (if not micro) level:

1. The breadth of deliverables you have to offer.
2. The Unique Selling Features of each or the WHAT factors of each.
3. The primary, secondary and tertiary facts or what factors around each deliverable.
4. Your primary, secondary and tertiary competitor's deliverables so you can differentiate between you and others in a meaningful manner when asked by a Customer or Prospect who may be considering multiple buying options.
5. An effective method to determine what the Customer's or Prospect's needs are, then only presenting the most powerful and appropriate solution deliverable to them.
6. How to not over-sell or present too many solutions, as this can overwhelm the other person and cause them to mentally disengage from the interaction
7. Whether you have a USF that can stand alone and is as powerful as that burger USF jingle used for decades.

Differentiating your offer by the tangibles offered is a hallmark trait of veteran successful sales professionals. Always know what you are saying before you say it, so you speak meaningfully and directly to the other person's needs.

Chapter 27

Performance-Driven Selling©
Differentiating Your
Offer/Approach via Unique
"Service" Feature Number Two

D ifferentiating your offer is another hallmark trait of veteran successful sales professionals. Sales is never a true 'apple-to-apple comparison.' When you can differentiate how your deliverable works versus other similar options, and then describe how you operate, deliver or are different, the competition pales in comparison.

While marketing has found that an organization or person can differentiate themselves in a marketplace by examining their USF #1; the selling world has also learned that sometimes an even greater differentiator is the sales professionals USF (Unique "Service" Feature) #2 .

USF #2 identifies all of the specific ways (tangible and intangible) in which your offer delivers unique value to the user. In essence, USF #2 centers on all of the things your offer does: the "how" factors.

Remember, USF #1 (Unique "Selling" Feature) is about the four core variables in the consumer's mind. What you sell/do that is:

1. *Better* than **what** they have now or is available in the marketplace; or
2. *Faster* than **what** they have now or is available in the marketplace; or
3. *Different* than **what** they have now or is available in the marketplace; or
4. *More Cost Effective* than **what** they have now or is available in the marketplace.

Many times in the marketplace, a Prospect/Customer may have a difficult time seeing how your differentiators perform genuinely differently than others'. When this happens, your offer may blend into the sea of options instead of standing out as **the** choice among options and offers.

With USF #2, the focus is on HOW you do what you do, allowing you to really differentiate yourself from your competitors.

You must have a depth of knowledge on all of the unique things that you represent. Knowing all of the unique "how" factors allows the sales professional to have an informed, educated and conversational engagement with Prospects/Customers. If a sales professional doesn't understand the "how" factors, then they will miss many selling opportunities.

USF #2 (remember Unique "Service" Feature) differentiates the above four core variables using powerful and appropriate HOW statements:

1. *It is Better* than **what** they have now or is available in the marketplace, and **how** it works better than any other market option; or

2. *It is Faster* than **what** they have now or is available in the marketplace, and **how** it works faster/more efficiently than any other market option; or

3. *It is Different* than **what** they have now or is available in the marketplace, and **how** it works differently than any other market option; or

4. *It is More Cost Effective* than **what** they have now or is available in the marketplace, and **how** it works more cost effectively than any other market option.

McDonald's differentiates itself in advertisements by using a "USF #2" when it says:

"Hold the pickles, hold the lettuce, special orders don't upset us, have it <u>your way</u>."

This statement differentiates them in the sea of fast-food hamburger options by communicating to the Prospects/Customers in their marketplace that if they want an individualized hamburger then they need to go to McDonald's. Do you have a Unique "Service" Feature that is as stand-alone and powerful as that McDonald's USF jingle used for decades?

As a sales professional, it is critical to know on a macro (if not micro) level:

1. The breadth of deliverables you have to offer and how each works.
2. The Unique "Selling" Features of each or the "how" factors of each.
3. The primary, secondary and tertiary facts, or the "what" factors, of each deliverable and how it serves others.
4. Your primary, secondary, and tertiary competitor's deliverables, so you can differentiate between yours and theirs in a meaningful manner when faced with a Customer or Prospect considering multiple buying options.
5. What the Customer's or Prospect's needs are (determined through vetting questions). Then only

131

presenting the most powerful and appropriate solution with an emphasis on your "how" factors.

Be careful not to over-sell or present too many solutions, as this can overwhelm the other person and cause them to mentally disengage from the interaction.

Chapter 28

**Performance-Driven Selling©
Showing the Prospect/Customer
Your Offer is Either Better,
Faster, More Cost Effective
or Different Than Anything
Else in the Marketplace**

While there are differing levels of decisions that a Prospect or Customer makes when going through the selling process, and there may even be multiple decision makers involved in the sales professional's Presentation, there are four ways in which a sales professional can make their offer stand apart from others.

As sales professionals, we must realize that every time a presentation is made, we must address one of (or a combination of) differentiators that consumers consider when selecting their purchasing options.

Whether all factors seem equal or not, people don't tend to make buying decisions or change a buying behavior unless you can demonstrate how your offer will make their life:

1. **Better** than their present state and better than the competition or other available choices.
2. **Faster** than their present state and better than the competition or other available choices.

3. **Uniquely Different** than their present state and better than the competition or other available choices.
4. **More Cost Effective** than their present state and better than the competition or other available choices. Everyone wants the biggest bang for their buck.

Evaluate the collateral informational or selling literature used, website or internet virtual posting, comments made, advertisements placed and Facts/Features presented in a selling process to recognize if, in fact, those efforts speak to one of the above differentiators.

There is no truly new anything in life. There are only adaptations, improvements, adjustments, modifications, etc., of existing products and services. To this point, the sales professional has to examine what they represent and ask themselves how their product or service compels another person to select their offer over other offers.

An easy way to answer that question is to ask probing, consultative (yet conversational) questions of the Prospect or Customer to determine what their core driving reason is for making a buying decision. Then, from the dominant information learned, speak to that sole point as your primary presentation. When you do so, do it in the most compelling manner possible so that the Prospect or Customer can really see why they will be better off selecting your option. You do this by demonstrating that your offer answers ... **"How does my offer do something either BETTER, FASTER, DIFFERENTLY or more COST EFFECTIVELY than anything else? And, if I can answer that, how is that answer so?"**

Successful selling involves communicating to the Prospect/Customer how your offer will be best for them based upon its unique Better, Faster, Different, Cost Effective variables. You can test these by evaluating your marketing materials. This can include the first landing pages of your website, any existing email proposals you have sent to a Prospect or Customer, new brochures, business cards, or informational media pieces. Print all of these items out in black and white ink.

Now grab four different color highlighter markers, one for each core decision driver. Let's say:

1. **BLUE** for **Better** than their present state; better than the competition or other available choices.
2. **GREEN** for **Faster** than their present state; better than the competition or other available choices.
3. **YELLOW** for **Uniquely Different** than their present state; better than the competition or other available choices.
4. **PINK** for **More Cost Effective** than their present state; better than the competition or other available choices.

Go through each document line-by-line and highlight accordingly any words, headlines, pictures, graphs, etc., that speak to your product or service being either Better, Faster, Different, or more Cost Effective. When you are done, any words not highlighted serve no motivating purpose in the mind of the receiver (Prospect/Customer).

Chapter 29

Performance-Driven Selling©
Seven Steps to Improved
Connection with the Other
Person through Improved
Listening Skills

It's been said that the greatest ability a person can have, even more so for a sales professional, is the ability to listen to another person without interrupting.

As sales professionals, the art of listening to the verbal and nonverbal language of the other person is critical in establishing rapport, engaging in needs analysis, and clearly determining if you have a solution for their immediate, intermediate, and long-term needs. It is difficult to listen to another person if your focus is not on that other person: if there are distractions, hidden agendas, frustrations, or a desire to finish with them and move on to another person or task.

Listening takes conscious effort. Realize that effective Presentations and increased sales effectiveness comes from your ability to clearly listen to the other person. You'll learn:

1. Do they think logically or emotionally? If you have had prior experience with personality/social style typing through instruments like Myers-Briggs, DISC, BANK, Hogan, Strength-Finders, Colors, etc., listen for these clues and blend your approach to each potential Customer, selling from their perspective, not yours.

2. Are they immediate-needs focused? Are they facing a time constraint that will influence their decision process?

3. Are they future-needs focused? Are they facing on-going and long-term time constraint needs that will influence their decision process?

4. Whether they are influenced or have any past experiences with you, your firm, other sales professionals, etc.

5. Where the common ground is between the two of you; and much more….

There are a lot of ways to improve one's listening ability. The following acronym will help you reduce your own talk time and tendency to interrupt, and improve your information-intake ability

Consider the following fundamental ways to engage and listen more effectively:

L = look and listen: see if nonverbal signals are consistent with verbal signals.

I = implied interest: by showing that you are genuinely interested in the other party they will become more comfortable with you, more relaxed, and thus, more engaging.

S = summarize: key points often to ensure that you are listening correctly, and conversely, that the points you make have value to the other person.

T = territorial: sensitivity to the other person in respect to their space, knowledge, beliefs, age, race, sex, profession, and station in life. Violation of any of these territories may cause the other person to tune you out. Likewise, if the other person in their dialogue violates one of your territories you may want to stop listening. Identify what has offended you and set that aside temporarily so you can focus on what they're saying.

E = empathetic position: this position must be taken by the sales professional with respect to what the other person says. Empathy implies that you understand; it doesn't imply that you agree with them or that they are right or wrong.

N = names, notes and nonverbal signals: there are three ways to use letter "N" as a listening technology tool. Using people's *names* in the conversation and in correspondence serves as a magnet to pull them and keep the dialogue personal; *note-taking* is a powerful tool for keeping control over one's mouth – if you have a tendency to talk too much or interrupt others, then start carrying a notepad, and when the other person talks, you take notes. It is physically impossible to write coherent notes and talk to someone at the same time. If you have a database or Customer relationship management system, capture detailed notes for your future reference and that of a colleague, should anyone else need to assist you with an account. The last way to use letter "N" as a listening tool is to watch the other person's *nonverbal* signals to ensure that they are consistent with their verbal signals; this is powerful.

S = **smile** (not smirk): it makes people warm up to you.

Far too many sales are lost because the sales professional talked too much and failed to listen effectively.

Effective listening will help you identify how many decision makers are involved in the decision to accept your offer. This is critical to making the sale. Through listening, you can identify what the dominant buying decisions of the other person(s) will be and the reasons behind their decisions – the why factors. These are among many critical factors necessary to making an effective presentation to the other party.

Listen for the dominant need or pain point that the other person shares or reveals through effective conversational engagement and listening. Then, start by making your case with a single dominant solution that you can provide. Listen effectively and then make your point by using their concerns, needs and words wrapped around your number one, most powerful solution. Once you've made the sale, you can go back and reinforce their decision with any additional value points.

Too much of a response and too many solutions can overwhelm the mind, and most often, when the mind becomes overwhelmed it shuts down and says 'no'.

Remember, listening is part art, part science and part self-control. Listening provides the path to interactive success with the other person now, and with additional follow-up, reinforcement to meet and sustain your relationship by fulfilling their on-going, intermediate and long-term needs. Through listening, if what you are doing is simple 'transactional' selling, you can make more transactional turns. Here you can quickly identify the upselling, cross-selling, and (when appropriate to keep and make the sale) downselling opportunities may be.

However, if what you are selling and working to achieve is a 'relationship selling' connection, then listening will allow you to uncover the building blocks of connectivity for a long-term relationship. This will bring you greater selling opportunities now and in the future and creating a great advocate who can become a lead-generating referral and source of market information.

Chapter 30

Performance-Driven Selling©
Improving Your Communication
Effectiveness:
The Art of Sending the
Correct Signal for Impact

Communication studies abound and while one report indicates how certain elements within a communication exchange influence its interpretation, another study says the opposite. Communication is both an art and a science, and we are constantly learning and improving. By understanding and applying three easy rules of communication, you can significantly increase the power of your next exchange, meeting presentation, and selling opportunity, whether written or spoken.

All communication experts agree that in both written and spoken communication exchanges there are three different elements:

1. There is a portion or percentage of the communication exchange sent that influences one's interpretation, solely based upon **WHAT** has been said.

2. There is a portion or percentage of the communication exchange sent that influences one's interpretation, solely based upon **WHY** the signal has been said.

3. There is a portion or percentage of the communication exchange sent that influences one's interpretation, solely based upon **HOW** the signal has been said.

As a sales professional, recognize that precisely what words and message you choose to send is critical. For this is the portion or percentage of the communication exchange that is rationalized for understanding. It is also the portion or percentage of the communication exchange that typically registers second overall. The "what" factors can make or break a communication exchange and those "what" factors can be:

1. The facts, logic, or data chosen by the sender and provided to the receiver from which to interpret.

2. The facts, data or logic should be matched to the recipient's ability to understand. Don't talk down to or above the receiver's reference about your message, and use facts, logic and data to make your point conversationally and non-combatively to the recipient.

3. The facts are typically those tangible elements connected to the communication signal, which the recipient processes from.

As the sales professional, you must also realize that the listener will put the message into its proper perspective based upon the supporting components sent that justify why the exchange is taking place or the urgency of the message. This may be done through nonverbal signals and/or additional influencers to the exchange. The "why" factors can make or break a communication exchange and those "why" factors can be:

1. The relational factors in the recipient's head that they reference in decoding your message.

2. The means in which the recipient rationalizes or reasons the context of the "what" factors, based upon their (the recipient's) reference or lack of reference to your facts, data and logic.

Ineffective communication exchanges are often due to poor transmission of that signal: What the human ear/eye registers before registering the "what" factor and how the signal is being sent. The "how" factors can make or break a communication exchange and those "how" factors can be one's:

1. Tone of voice or messaging
2. Pitch of voice or messaging
3. Pace of voice or messaging
4. Volume of voice or messaging
5. Accent of voice or messaging
6. Intonation of voice or messaging

As a sales professional, realize that while you may spend significant time working on exactly what to say to a Prospect/Customer, there also needs to be attention and sensitivity paid to how and why that signal will be sent.

Sales professionals can authenticate their message and allow for adjustments to the "how", "what" and "why" factors by recognizing that there are also double standards that can make or break dialogues, as well.

1. If a man is assertive in his tone of voice when communicating, many times it is acceptable; but if not, most would label that communication behavior as aggressive, pushy or a jerk – all logical rationalizations.

2. However, if a woman communicates assertively, in many instances she will be heard not as assertive, aggressive or pushy, but rather as a domineering individual – or a word that rhymes with "itch" – an

emotional rationalization. The analysis is more emotionally based than logic based, and when one mentally reaches this conclusion, there will be an instant communication breakdown.

Is this a double standard? Yes. Is this reality? Yes. The point here is not to debate the merits of the signal influence, rather recognize how people actually register signals. Effective communicators are sensitive to both what is being said, why it is being said and, most importantly, how it is being said.

By understanding and applying these three easy rules of communication exchanges, you can significantly increase the power of your next exchange, meeting presentation, or selling opportunity, whether written or spoken.

Section III
Accelerating the Fundamentals

Chapter 31

Performance-Driven Selling©
Using Rule 1/52/X™ Allows
You to Remain Connected
to Your Market & Keeps
Your Sales Funnel Full

Great sales professionals aren't born. There is planned strategic work and daily tactical efforts that lead to consistent sales and success in the field. Your job as a sales professional is to recognize the differing daily efforts (work product) that can assist in generating inquiries from targeted demographics, which can result in a sales Presentation and subsequent increased Closing ratios. This same daily effort (work product) can be strategically adapted into your daily routine to gain market awareness and connectivity in a virtual manner when you can't physically be everywhere you need to be for success.

Realize that during the windows of downtime in your sales day, there are productive, constructive activities that should dominate your schedule. As an example, unless you have set callbacks and scheduled appointments on a Monday morning (and in some cases on a Monday at any time), attempting to make cold calls or initiate new activities on a Monday can be counterproductive.

I have learned that Mondays can become your secret strategic weapon to productive selling activities for Tuesday through Friday of every week, with one strategic adjustment – deploy **Rule 1/52/X™**.

The strategic implications of this tool can be monumental when used in alignment with your annual sales business planning. This includes every KPI (Key Performance Indicator) within every week and day of critical action steps (don't know what is trying to be said) for measurable and meaningful ROI.

One way to turn cold calls into warm calls (most sales professionals would rather have their teeth pulled without pain-numbing medicines than make cold calls on a daily basis) is by deploying Rule 1/52/X™. No matter what business you are in, the ability to develop deeper relationships with existing Customers is the fastest way to your selling success. However, at some point, you must engage people that do not know you to keep your selling funnel/pipeline flowing and new sales (sales, enlistments, donors, etc.) taking place.

Rule 1/52/X™ allows you to stimulate consistent inquiries about your services/products; to reach out to never before contacted suspects or Prospects; to make the introduction of you-to-them in a non-threatening manner; and to ensure that your Sales Funnel or Sales Pipeline always remains full of leads.

So, what is Rule 1/52/X™? It is a systematic approach (either manual or automated) that compliments your selling effort with manageable marketing efforts.

I learned early in my career the self-discipline it takes to always be feeding your selling funnel (lead generation). If I did not do this or forgot to stay on top of lead generation, I would find myself working one hot lead through the selling process and when it either closed or blew up, all of my leads were cold or non-existent. As I got older and led and observed selling organizations, I realized that this is a consistent behavior flaw with most selling professionals and their organizations.

If you expect to see increased and steady ROI, set an auto reminder in your smartphone system or database system to remind you and hold you accountable to the deployment of this concept as detailed below.

Rule 1/52/X™ explained ...

> **1 = Represents the actions that should take place every Monday or the first day of your weekly seven-day selling cycle.** Thus, the first day/week of each month you focus on lead generation, whether that includes new or reconnection activities.

> **52 = Represents a consistent approach for every week of the year.** You commit to do this every week for at least 52 weeks before you make an annual selling review of ROI.

> **X = Represents a targeted demographic and number of outbound contacts to be initiated that week.** Example: Identify the best 50 suspects that you want to meet, or your top/best x-Prospects that you want to make a specific offer to, or your top/best x-Customers (active or inactive) that you want to place a specific offer in front of, etc.

Building rapport, establishing relationships, maintaining relationships and establishing your brand presence requires, among many factors, your ability to 'meaningfully' get and stay connected to the marketplace.

Your ability to identify the appropriate demographic constituents (existing Customers, core VIPs, critical COIs, lost or inactive Customers that you want to reconnect with, a new suspect or Prospect pool that you need to penetrate, etc.) and select an appropriate quantity of contacts to whom you can send a marketing pulse on Monday. Teeing up people to make outbound contact with on subsequent days, along with your other business-development responsibilities, ensures that you are always seeding and feeding your selling-funnel initiatives, driving people to your business.

The specific contact action can vary greatly and could have a powerful call-to-action message. It should a direct marketing approach that is as targeted and as personalized as possible. Examples:

1. A handwritten notecard with handwritten envelope (studies reveal handwritten envelopes are opened first in a stack of mail and handwritten notes are read from beginning to end and not scanned). Always include several of your business cards.

2. A personal letter with a suggested approach via one of your products/services that the contact may not be aware of. Always include several of your business cards.

3. An email announcement, offer, request, press release, etc.

4. A posting to any one of your social media platforms, follower groups, etc.

5. A faxable/e-faxable note and a fax-back response request form for more information or requested follow-up.

6. A direct mail card, letter, or campaign announcing who you are or a great new product or feature that is available and ways for them to find out more information or contact you.

7. A copy of any press releases or press clippings that may intrigue the contact and stimulate them to contact you for more information.

8. A social media video message or directed targeted YouTube posting.

9. A directed text message with a short, powerful, call to action.

10. An update on a Customer who had a similar problem to the contact's. Share the story of their newfound successes from your offering.

Brainstorm with your fellow sales professionals differing ways to contact suspects, Prospects, Customers, and inactive clients. Also brainstorm powerful messages to include.

Now cold calls become warm calls. A sales professional can now make an outbound call to a suspect, Prospect or Customer and the call can go like:

"Hello, this is _____ with _____. I sent you a recent note on _____. Have you had the opportunity to read it?"

1. If the answer is yes, then proceed with your conversational sales process. This warm approach won't catch anyone off guard as to who you are why you are contacting them.

2. If the answer is no, then "That's alright, why I sent it to you is…." and this is still a warm approach, as it places the focus of the conversation on what was sent and they can refer to it while you are talking or after you have talked with them.

Now accelerate your selling success and increase your market opportunities by strategically applying the Rule 1-52-X™ as a CAMPAIGN approach to your database. This will allow you to reach a wider market that neither you nor your competition has probably ever engaged on a regular basis. Do not make this a major work product event. Simply weave this into your normal, and even unexpected, daily activities so it becomes an administrative strategic event flow. Campaign ideas:

1. Monday – engage a portion of your regular client base or your top 1-percent (primary) profile Prospect lists with a messaging reason to want to talk with you, thereby feeding your funnel. Make a commitment to make a follow-up courtesy call within the coming days to engage them in a consultative rapport-building conversation. On the following Monday, continue on to other names on the same demographic lists that you have not been able to reach. continue onward until that list is complete. Then re-loop again, and again, and again.

2. Tuesday – engage a portion of your regular client base or your secondary profile Prospect lists with a messaging reason to want to talk with you, thereby feeding your funnel. Make a commitment to make a follow-up courtesy call within the coming days to engage them in a consultative rapport-building conversation or invite them to an engagement event. On the following Tuesday, continue on to other names on the same demographic lists that you have not been able to reach, and onward until that list is complete. Then re-loop again, and again, and again.

3. Wednesday - engage your COI/VIP base list(s) with a messaging reason to want to talk with you, thereby feeding your funnel. Make a commitment to make a follow-up courtesy call within the coming days to engage them in a consultative rapport-building conversation; cultivate a consistent working relationship with them that generates consistent lead flow and market intelligence; or invite them to an engagement event. On the following Wednesday, continue on to other names on the same demographic lists that you have not been able to reach, and onward until that list is complete. Then re-loop again, and again, and again.

4. Thursday - contact the list of all Prospects you have engaged over the past 24 months and lost, were unable to convert or dropped off your radar. Send them a messaging reason to want to talk with you, thereby feeding your funnel. Make a commitment to make a follow-up courtesy call within the coming days to engage them in a consultative rapport-building conversation or to invite them to an engagement event; On the following Thursday, continue on to other names on same demographic lists that you have not been able to reach, and onward until that list is complete. then re-loop again, and again, and again.

You can automate this process or operate off of an Excel spreadsheet; whatever works best for you. Your ability to remain connected on a regular basis will allow you to elevate yourself and your organization as a real brand in the marketplace's mind.

Rule 1/52/X™ helps fill your individual or organization's Sales Funnel. It may stimulate some contacts to call you and it may even add to your bottom line, merely from a simple letter and postage stamp. Low-cost marketing, high-yield sales.

Chapter 32

**Performance-Driven Selling©
Leveraging Existing Business
Relationships for Greater
Business Opportunities …
aka 100% of 100% Strategy**

One of the most overlooked business development areas of professional selling is the existing client.

With the exception of those rare instances in which a selling situation may merely be 'transactional' with transit Customers, the fastest way to increase sales volume is to start with existing clients (especially satisfied Customers). Most sales professionals fail to see the totality of business opportunities that may be directly connected with every individual client in their portfolio. Most selling organizations and individuals are trained to make the sale and then go after the next Prospect or suspect in their marketplace. This has become the norm in the B2B, B2C and C2C marketplace, whether in traditional selling or virtual e-Commerce selling.

Once the hard work of building rapport and trust with the other person and, in this case the Customer, has been accomplished, your ability to leverage that relationship should be foremost on your mind – serving others by serving your contact-client relationship.

Think of your daily schedule, marketing and advertising efforts, client-development contact initiatives, all sales-funnel or sales-pipeline endeavors. Consider this:

1. **100% of 100%** - Until I have connected with 100 percent of existing clients and ensure that I have educated or provided an opportunity for them to participate in 100 percent of my deliverables. I will not place any energy on non-Customer endeavors.

2. **100% of 100%** - Then ask yourself, how do I consultatively engage 100 percent of my existing clients and build a trust-based relationship with each of them. This will allow me to engage them for referrals from their contacts, clients, vendors, and network who may be viable clients.

You can even design an advocacy/referral program, (as ethically appropriate for your demographic market segmentation) whereby you can reward or compensate your clients for new business they connect you to.

3. **100% of 100%** - If you are a membership-based organization, ask yourself how do I consultatively engage 100 percent of my existing members and build a trust-based relationship with each of them This will allow me to engage them for referrals from their contacts, clients, vendors, and network who may be viable clients.

Sales professionals need to ask existing clients enough questions to determine what products/services in the line-up of offerings will address the client's immediate needs. Also, what products/services will be necessary sequentially in your line-up of offerings to get the client from where they are today (immediate need) to where they say they want to be in the future (long-term need)?

By knowing a client's short-term and long-term goals, you can serve as consultant to a client's success and guide them toward smarter purchasing decisions, increased purchasing decisions and more profitable purchasing decisions. A powerful way to gain this insight is from your client's Mission Statement: what they deem important and where they indicate they, as an organization, are going.

Recognize the time it takes to find a new suspect, convert them into a Prospect, communicate and entice them into a Sales Presentation and close a new Customer out of that relationship. It is extremely more expensive when compared to cultivating more business from existing clients – **100% of 100%**.

Another way that sales professionals can cultivate additional business from existing clients, beyond expanding the level/volume of utilization and consummation of products/services by the current client, is to utilize them as a conduit to other Customers within their same organization/place/family/group or from within their network. Every existing client breaks down into one of three transaction statuses.

1. Some will be merely Customers and would rather blend away.
2. A second group may be a Customer by default and will not want to assist you in any endeavor.
3. A third subgroup will always be raving fans, advocates, allies, and Centers-of-Influence if you just actively engage them and give them the opportunity to further serve you.

By identifying this third subgroup, you can shorten that Sales Presentation curve of finding and making the next sale by having qualified leads from these fans.

Brainstorm an example of one of your organization's existing clients. See how many other potential buyers there could be within that one point-of-contact that you are not presently in dialogue with. The leverage here, in contacting that new potential buying contact, is that there is already a relationship between you and their organization and that helps to ensure that you are a credible option.

We are conditioned to see our market through the lens of our predecessor or the organization's lens of past selling history. I learned this years ago, not by design, but mere accident. I had a client within an organization, at a specific business level. What I offered made sense for what was needed and that client bought from me. When he got promoted, he bought from me again from another business unit that I had previously never even considered as a Prospect. Then, I learned that he was a member of several organizations, some connected to his employment organization and others that were not. He recommended me and they bought from me, as well. Next, I identified vendors that supplied his association and business, and they bought. What I learned from this one relationship is that there are multiple layers of possible business transaction opportunities, and these transactions happened only because of the relationship.

Now, let's apply this concept and strategy within and throughout your organization. Every leader at every level and in every business unit should create a best-in-class work area that attracts and retains great talent. If done, then everyone would be excited to generate quality leads on a regular basis.

You can dramatically increase sales effectiveness by cultivating or mining existing client relationships for additional business opportunities and transactions, while at the same time focusing efforts on looking for new clients altogether.

Refer to Chapter 38 for more **100% of 100%** applications to selling success as it relates to where your energy should be now and later.

Chapter 33

Performance-Driven Selling©
Getting Referrals from
Every New Client,
Customer/Recruitment

Studies show that it takes significantly more time, energy and money to solicit, earn and on-board new business from individuals and organizations that are not presently doing business with you, than it does to cultivate qualified Prospects and clients from your existing network. In fact, TARP recalibrated the selling world back in the 1970s with its ground-breaking research that indicated businesses can increase profitability five times faster through present Customer interaction than any other endeavor done to find new business. Yet somehow, this is most often overlooked.

Despite all of the evidence, it is still the norm of sales professionals, sales managers, and organizations to focus on gaining new clients, ignoring their selling pipeline and existing relationships.

While new clients are the lifeblood of any business, maintaining healthy productive relationships with existing clients will do more for building a solid business base and revenue streams. **Sales professionals need to review their present business**

activities to answer:

1. What percentage of my work is centered on cultivating additional business from existing clients? _____%

2. What percentage of my work is centered on getting to know existing clients to either ask them for referrals or to allow for the client to give me referrals? _____%

3. What percentage of my existing clients, if ranked from #1 to #10, could I write a short story about, based upon what I know about them? _____%

4. What percentage of my existing clients, if ranked from #1 to #10, do I know enough about their deliverables to recommend qualified leads to them? _____%

5. What percentage of my work is centered on building my business base by identifying and working to get new clients? _____%

These are powerful questions to ask yourself to determine if you have been "leaving money on the table" – a term used for not actively working every account to do all of the business possible with them.

Building Customer loyalty comes out of many acts, including genuinely taking care of a Customer's immediate needs and doing the same for their close friends and business associates – it makes them look good and endears you to them.

As a sales professional, you must recognize the opportunities or best times in a sales transaction to hint, suggest or request great referrals from a satisfied Customer.

Referrals can come in many ways:

1. **Verbal recommendation to call someone specific** – Get the name at the precise moment it is offered, write it down along with a few quick facts about them, (refer to the Stack-N-Link model in previous chapter to ask the types of questions that will help you learn more about the new suggested contact).

2. **Email, telephone, written options** – When a suggested name is given, request that the Customer send that data back to you when they get home or to work via alternate communication channels. You can always follow-up with the Customer afterwards via these same channels to remind them of the offer. These channels are easy to use and non-threatening to either party, as there is no live conversation. It is acceptable to remind a Customer of an offer to recommend, but don't hassle them.

3. **Victory letter & social media** – Ask the Customer who sings your praise to put those words into a letter for you to share with other potential Customers. As you're having this dialogue, transition into a subtle question, "Are there people that you know that I should send your letter to?" This can be used in your collateral materials, on your social media platforms, website, and as reinforcement marketing vehicles in the selling communication exchange processes.

4. **Customer literature** – Ask if the Customer has any organizational printed materials for their Customers where they list benefits or accomplishments that you contributed to. Have them reference your name (personal or business) or include a picture of you (personal or business) as a preferred partner, vendor, suppliers, etc., and then get a copy.

5. **Ask while completing application** - The best time to ask for a referral is when you have just provided a solution to a Prospect's need. With that Prospect now an

excited new client/Customer, ask for the name of anyone that person knows who you should be talking to next.

6. **Frequent Customer loyalty referral program** – You can create and incentivize present Customers to share their excitement with those they know. Offer an incentive for referring them to you and your organization.

7. **Regular follow-up connectivity** – It should be an SOP of every professional selling individual and their organization to have a system by which you can stay connected with Customers after the sale is made and the goods are delivered. Every month or quarter, as appropriate to your business, you should have some sort of a touchpoint back to the Customer. These touchpoints do not have to be follow-up selling initiatives, (it's actually best if they are not always selling contacts, rather service connectivity follow-ups). Within these touchpoints you can always have a bounce-back referral opportunity.

Use the positive words of praise from your present Customers as supplements to any mailers you or your sales professionals do, (and this could be a great rotation into your Rule 1/52/X™, to display in wall hangings, display books on tables, reprints, inclusion in newsletters, faxables, e-Marketing, social media, publications and blogs, etc.).

Sometimes, the best silent sales assistants you can have are the words of praise from a satisfied Customer. Leverage those words with people that directly know the Customer in question. A second way to leverage these words is to identify all "like" points of contact to the Customer and place the words in front of them.

A great way to complete the sales cycle is to send every Customer, regardless of the amount of the transaction, a follow-up handwritten Thank-you note. Include with it an extra business card (ask them to share your business card with someone they would like to share their experience with) and a simple request to call you with the name(s) of anyone they know that you should contact. Every one of these contacts will not yield feedback, but many will, and every one will leave a Customer with one more positive impression of you or your organization.

Chapter 34

Performance-Driven Selling©
Cultivating New Business
Opportunities from
Dead/Lost Account Contacts
via the BLENDS™ Formula

Every business across the globe has one... it is that file cabinet stuffed full of inactive clients or an electronic database file of the same – some for legitimate reasons and many for reconcilable reasons.

These are very possible acres of diamonds just waiting to be re-shined and engaged with once again.

You must recognize the profitable potential of those inactive clients that everyone knows are present, yet no one wants to go after. So before you contact them, do some research. The analytics will typically reveal that they left for one of (or a combination of) four core reasons.

Customers leave/become inactive because of ...

1. Financial Reasons – They felt that they could get a better buy somewhere else; the value proposition for the price point did not have a meaningful enough impact on them to remain a Customer; their budgets restricted them at

the time to remain with you; etc. ... Time may have changed this reason.

2. A Product/Service Needs Change – They believed, (sometimes rightfully so) you could not meet their existing or new needs. Time may have changed this reason.

3. Perception – They felt that as a vendor, you didn't appreciate their level of business and that they became a mere number on the roster of many clients; there is a misconnect in their minds as to how they were being treated or where your business was going and that is did not include them. Time may have changed this reason.

4. Communication Issues – There was a series of miscommunications, negative communications, poor communications, a lack of communication, too much communication, non-appreciative communication, or unaligned communication from the organization that is in conflict with the Customer's values or beliefs. Time may have changed this reason.

If a sales professional analyzes a lost account for one of these four basic reasons, they will likely be able to determine why that client became inactive. If the client left for legitimate reasons that remain true, you may not want to reach out. However, if that account became inactive for reconcilable reasons, go after that client with the BLENDS model.

Recognize which approach would be most productive in engaging that inactive client and initiating a healthy new dialogue. Use any one of these strategies of the BLENDS Model for that added reconnection:

B – Directs you to contact an inactive account, which may require a lot of energy. A good time for this is immediately after you have had an interaction with an exceedingly positive client. Use that contact as an added BOOST to reconnect with a lost account, as your enthusiasm can be contagious.

Maybe you just received a powerful email endorsing or praising your efforts; you could use this to motivate you forward on the identified lost account contact. You could also include the email as an attachment or embedded reference.

L – Send that inactive account a new LETTER introducing yourself as a new point of contact and what you have to offer that could increase the quality of their life. In this letter, you can share testimonials from current happy clients, share collateral information, brochures, press clippings, etc., and something with a call-to-action to raise the recipient's level of interest in the hope that they accept your inbound call or even reach out to you for a conversation.

E – EXAMINE the EVIDENCE as to why they stopped being a Customer. Set your personal emotion and bias aside and read the historical documents from the lost Customer's perspective. Based upon those findings, determine how you could assist them in today's marketplace based upon the products/services you now offer.

N – Offer to perform an account NEEDS Analysis/Audit for them free of charge. Many new clients can be gained, and many inactive clients can be regained, by you partnering with them to provide your expert analysis on how to proceed, operate, what to produce, how to produce, and what to be preparing for in today's market, etc.

D – DO SOMETHING for them. Contact them, introduce yourself to them and offer to do something for them that only you can do and that would have value for them.

S – If you can offer something of value to them, provide them with a current SAMPLE of what you do that they may not be aware of.

Blending into your typical daily routine some activity in the area of account redevelopment is a great way to breathe life back into those dead accounts. Realize that the dead accounts have been dead for some time due to the lack of anyone attempting a concentrated campaign of working on them. Odds are that after a few attempts using this strategy you will give up on them, as well – but the true sales professionals will pace themselves and blend this account development work into their Sales Funnel along with all other account development activities. Deploy this strategy in concert with Rule 1-52-X™, also presented within the Performance-Driven Selling® theories.

Chapter 35

Performance-Driven Selling©
Cross-Selling for Increased
Business Opportunities

Cross-selling is the fluid ability of a sales professional to meet a Prospect's/Customer's immediate needs, while mentally evaluating other parallel products or services to meet future needs.

It is the sale after the sale, or the service after the service, that builds a deeper relationship and interaction. This serves to build the connectivity that attracts and keeps Customers and generates the energy with a Customer to become your advocate.

You need to always be on the lookout for relevant selling opportunities in each transaction to present to a contact. You want to be able to evaluate during the given transaction what other offers you have that can enhance, improve and compliment your existing presentation/offer. You do this as a service to the buyer, and not as a mere means of making another sale for the sale's sake.

For example, if a person is buying a new tie, you might ask if they have a tie tack. At which point the Customer may say no and may also say he doesn't need or want one. Cross-selling would then go into motion with the sales professional saying something like:

"I can appreciate how you feel. The reason I ask is that I wear a tie tack/tie clasp with all my ties and as you can see, you can't see it. I wear my tie clasp under the tie and clip it against my inner tie and shirt to hold it in one place and now the tie always stay perfectly aligned and no tie jewelry is visible, as I don't like them outwardly visible either."

This intrigue may work powerfully at getting the buyer to now accept another product to compliment their initial purchase.

The same holds true if you are engaging a Prospect about joining/enlisting in your organization, by asking the following at the time of the presentation:

"As you consider this decision to join/enlist, there are probably a few great people that look to you for direction and that you would probably enjoy sharing this experience with. Who should we talk to after we finalize this paper work?"

Or

"Let's get you onboarded into the organization and then let's set a time for us to reconnect. At that time, it will be appropriate to outline several other benefits you can draw upon as a member of the organization. ..."

You must recognize the appropriate Cross-selling items or which products/services you offer that have obvious Cross-selling opportunity and role play some of those as examples with another person to build your confidence and proficiency. Show them some examples using the Five-Step Selling Process (Claim-Fact/Feature-Benefit-Naildown sequence).

Every Customer contact is an opportunity to meet their needs. If you do a thorough job in the Inquiry stage of the selling process, (uncovering their immediate, intermediate and future needs) then in the Presentation stage, several options can be presented.

Instead of "you may need this," the conversation may be more like, "along with this, you also may want to consider getting this and this with it."

You are always looking at the totality of needs that can be fulfilled with the totality of products/services you represent, all with the best interest of the Customer in mind.

If you are presenting the purchase of a skill development workshop to a Prospect and they say yes, then you would potentially Cross-sell them on purchasing books or audio tapes/CDs or even an online subscription to a self-development portal platform for everyone as an after-workshop reinforcement to key content information.

You should always be thinking of additional opportunities with every transaction. However, making the options available at the time of the initial transaction is not always the best window of additional selling opportunity. So, this may be merely the time when you make a reference for later discussion. You can also cross-sell after the transaction, as well.

Cross-selling can take on many different forms. It can be a valuable and legitimate reason for continued follow-up with clients, ensuring they are aware of additional ways to enhance their last transaction with you, and thus, build a better and deeper relationship with them. Consider reconnections:

1. You can use new product/service introductions as a reason to stay in contact with new and established Customers to let them know of new offerings; see if they would like to make that purchase, upgrade, etc.

2. Then use this legitimate reconnection as an opportunity, (when appropriate) to solicit referrals from them and their vast network, personal and professional.

3. Leverage yourself as a Subject-Matter-Expert and reflect on ways to share your unique industry experience, marketplace opportunities, or perspectives on how to utilize your organization's deliverables more effectively so the client can gain additional ROIs.

4. Leverage your colleagues as Subject-Matter-Experts and reflect on ways to share their unique industry experience, marketplace opportunities, or perspectives on how to utilize your organization's deliverables more effectively so the client can gain additional ROIs.

5. Leverage yourself as a Subject-Matter-Expert, always reflecting on ways to strategically share your database for introductions within the industry and marketplace opportunities so the client can gain additional ROIs.

6. Use your existing relationship as an opportunity to explore other services, deliverables or horizontal add-ons that you may have that can enhance their professional needs for an upgrade in the relationship.

7. Constantly evaluate the marketplace for other suppliers, vendors, manufacturers, etc. who may compliment the product/service you are providing to your client. When your client acquires that deliverable, the complimentary product/service will enhance what they offer to their subsequent Customers and may even enhance their marketplace position.

8. Examine the form of the deliverable that you are providing in the marketplace. Then evaluate whether you have or could create a new deliverable that enhances

what the client is doing with you. This cross-sale strengthens your relationship and generates additional revenue streams.

Example: If you are engaged in professional-personal development by attending a human capital development onsite training program and gain value from that experience, this would be the initial sale activity. Then, if there were online learning and development portal self-driven courseware programs, and the person you did or are doing business with lets you know about this additional opportunity as an additional way to increase your skill set, and thus marketplace value, you would want to know and consider this. This would be the first follow-up cross-selling opportunity.

Then, sometime in the future, if there were a release of new resources, (book, audio, online program, coaching, mastermind collaboration groups, improved live onsite program, etc.) these would all be additional Cross-selling opportunities.

You could design regular touchpoints to keep your name in front of the client or marketplace through penning regular, high-value, content-rich articles or an article series/column that can be delivered via social media/internet subscription, (free or for a fee), or traditional hard copy distribution that reinforce the spirit, theme, reason for the initial client interaction ...

Completely fulfilling a Customer's needs with all products/services offered by your organization/department is the responsibility of every sales professional and sales leader.

Another means to fulfilling legitimate Prospect/Customer needs from a cross-selling perspective may be to deploy the *Business Integration Grid* ™ (BIG), discussed in Chapter 38. Consider:

1. Connecting your clients and the services or deliverables they need from you with another product or service that

a non-competing entity or vendor provides. Now imagine you had forged a referral relationship with those non-competing entities or vendors (partnerships, collaborations, alliance-partners). You could recommend them to serve your clients' needs and generate an additional free revenue stream to you and your organization.

2. Now, explore the same BIG model in reverse, looking at the contacts and Customers that these partners already have relationships with. Brainstorm the massive business development opportunities that may be present and analyze which services or deliverables you have that they would need. Then build a campaign to connect to those contacts and Customers based on your referral relationship with those non-competing entities or vendors. Based off of the relationship you have and the trust factor established with them, and their respective trust factor to their clients, you could now recommend services and deliverables that would serve them in their needs and at the same time generate an additional free revenue stream to you and your organization – and additional revenue streams to those partnered organizations.

I was dining at a restaurant in Austin, Texas. Customers included conference-goers and vacationers in the community, as well as locals. In the lobby, they had a large caldron where people were dropping in their business cards. There must have been thousands. I asked management what they were doing with them... nothing – ouch. They also had a smartphone app people could download for access to the venue's products. They weren't utilizing these contacts either.

The missed opportunities for Cross-selling (and even upselling) opportunities were limitless.

1. The store had an onsite gift shop with customized items just feet away from their entrance and the caldron of

business cards. These could be pre- and post-follow-up sale items or give aways.

2. The restaurant could look at their business analytics and determine what days and times they had low, slow sales and gear marketing campaigns and incentives to local traffic to increase business during those hours and days, to increase overall revenue streams.

3. They could have a marketing staffer or team analyze the business cards for the types of people, titles, and organizations that patronize the restaurant and create targeted marketing campaigns, catering business opportunities, or sales offerings.

These are just some of the easy examples of ways to cross-sell. Again, completely fulfilling a Customer's needs with all products/services offered by your organization/department, and from those that you can pre-vet as legitimate, is the responsibility of a professional sales representative and sales leader.

Chapter 36

Performance-Driven Selling©
Upselling for Business-Development
Relationships

Upselling is the fluid ability of a sales professional to meet a Prospect's/Customer's immediate needs, while mentally evaluating other products or services they represent to determine if there are more efficient ways in which they can serve the Customer.

The ability to recognize what the real immediate and long-term need of a Prospect/Customer is, and how you can best satisfy that need, may in some situations require you to invest more time with them.

As a sales professional, you must always be on the lookout for relevant Upselling opportunities in each transaction. The sales professional should evaluate during each transaction if there is an Upselling opportunity to a better product/service (special, new, improved, discontinued, rebated, better profit margin items) they have that can enhance, improve and complement the existing purchase. A professional sales representative does this as a service to the buyer and not as a mere means of making another sale for the sale's sake.

In exploring relevant Upselling opportunities, consider that the buying decisions of a Prospect/Customer are weighted based upon needs. There are four core needs a Prospect/Customer may have when making a buying decision (or if they are considering affiliating with or joining your organization). These are:

1. Financial
2. Technical
3. Use (implementation/application)
4. Advocate (vanity/ego)

Simple Example - A man is buying a new suit. The sales professional might ask him how he plans to wear it. If the answer is for basic occasional wear, then any suit will probably do. However, if the man (Customer to be) indicates that it will be worn frequently in front of other professionals and he will be very active while wearing it, the sales professional may have information that can be used to justify a better, more expensive suit.

Recruitment Example – You have just recruited an individual to your organization. You must make them aware of services, programs, positions, jobs, formal/informal educational growth opportunities available within the organization. This can provide both Upselling opportunities and a means of greater commitment by the new member to your organization.

Now, an even better example of an Upselling opportunity in the recruitment example would have been to have considered, at the outset, if the new Prospect could not only join, but become a referring advocate. Then they may be able to come in at an elevated place in your organization (more rank, let's say) with more compensation.

As a sales professional, you must recognize the appropriate Upselling items or which products/services you offer that have obvious Upselling opportunity.

Every Customer contact is an opportunity to meet their needs. If the sales professional does a thorough job uncovering the

Customer's needs (immediate and future) during the Inquiry stage of the selling process, then in the Presentation stage, Upselling options can be presented.

Instead of, "this will address your needs", the conversation may be more like, "you may want to consider this instead of that, as this will do a much better job at..."

Always be looking at the totality of needs that can be fulfilled with the totality of products/services you represent, all with the best interest of the Customer in mind.

Another example: If you are presenting an educational or motivational keynote speaker for a conference to a Prospect and they say yes, then you would potentially Upsell them on purchasing a break-out workshop while your speaker is there. Or the investment by them or a sponsor of supplemental resources for everyone in the audience, such as books or online subscriptions to developmental services. Now you have gone from one small sale to two sales with greater revenue opportunity, and thus, increased profitability.

As a sales professional, you should always be thinking of greater opportunities with every transaction. To make those options available at the time of the initial transaction is the best window of Upselling opportunity. You can also Upsell after the transaction, as well, using new product/service introductions as a reason to contact recent Customers.

Upselling can take many different forms. It can be a valuable and legitimate reason for continued follow-up with clients, ensuring they are aware of additional ways to enhance their last transaction with you, thereby building a better and deeper relationship with them. Consider reconnections:

1. You can use new product/service introductions as a reason to stay in contact with new and established

Customers. Let them know of new offerings, upgrades, etc., and if you can work the financials so that what they previously purchased can be credited in some degree towards their next purchase, you earn even greater respect and leverage.

2. Then use this legitimate reconnection as an opportunity, as and when appropriate, to solicit referrals from them and their vast network, personal and professional.

3. Leverage yourself as a Subject-Matter-Expert, always reflecting on ways to share your unique industry experience, marketplace opportunities, or perspectives on how to utilize your organization's deliverables more effectively so the client can gain additional ROIs.

4. Leverage your colleagues as Subject-Matter-Experts and always be reflecting on ways to share their unique industry experience, marketplace opportunities, or perspectives on how to utilize your organization's deliverables more effectively so the client can gain additional ROIs.

5. Leverage yourself as a Subject-Matter-Expert, always reflecting on ways to share your database strategically for introductions within the industry and marketplace so the client can gain additional ROIs.

6. Use your existing relationship as an opportunity to explore other services, deliverables or horizontal add-ons that you may have that can enhance their professional needs for an upgrade in the relationship.

7. Always evaluate the marketplace for other suppliers, vendors, manufacturers, etc. who may have a deliverable that can be added or combined to what you

sell to enhance what they offer to their Customers or their marketplace position.

8. Examine the form of the deliverable that you are providing in the marketplace and any specific Customer, then evaluate whether you have, or could create, a new deliverable as an upgrade to enhance what the client is doing with you. This upsale strengthens your relationship and generates additional revenue streams.

   Example: If you are engaged in professional-personal development by attending a human capital development onsite training program and gain value from that experience, this would be the initial sale activity. Then, if there were online learning and development portal self-driven courseware programs, and the person you did or are doing business with lets you know about this additional opportunity as an additional way to increase your skill set, and thus marketplace value, you would want to know and consider this. This would be the first follow-up upselling opportunity.

Sometime in the future, if there were a release of new resources, (book, audio, online program, coaching, mastermind collaboration groups, improved live onsite program, etc.) these would all be additional Upselling opportunities.

You could design regular touchpoints to keep your name in front of the client or marketplace by penning regular, high-value, content-rich articles or an article series/column that can be delivered via social media/internet subscription, (free or for a fee), or traditional hard copy distribution that reinforce the spirit, theme, reason for the initial client interaction…

Another means to fulfilling legitimate Prospect/Customer needs from an Upselling perspective may be to deploy the *Business Integration Grid* ™ (BIG), discussed in Chapter 38. Consider:

1. Connecting your clients and the services or deliverables they need from you with another product or service that a non-competing entity or vendor provides. Now imagine you had forged a referral relationship with those non-competing entities or vendors (partnerships, collaborations, alliance-partners). You could recommend them to serve your clients' needs and generate an additional free revenue stream to you and your organization.

2. Now, explore the same BIG model in reverse, looking at the contacts and Customers that these partners already have relationships with. Brainstorm the massive business development opportunities that may be present and analyze which services or deliverables you have that they would need. Then build a campaign to connect to those contacts and Customers based on your referral relationship with those non-competing entities or vendors. Based off of the relationship you have and the trust factor established with them, and their respective trust factor to their clients, you could now recommend services and deliverables that would serve them in their needs and at the same time generate an additional free revenue stream to you and your organization – and additional revenue streams to those partnered organizations.

Completely fulfilling a Customer's needs with all products/services offered by your organization/department is the responsibility of every sales professional and sales leader.

Chapter 37

Performance-Driven Selling©
Downselling to Better Serve
Your Client Relationships

Downselling is the fluid ability of a sales professional to meet a Prospect's/Customer's immediate needs, while mentally evaluating other products or services they represent to determine if there are more efficient ways in which they can further meet a Prospect's/Customer's needs in the future.

As a sales professional, you must always be on the lookout for relevant Downselling opportunities in each transaction. Overselling a Prospect/Customer for a one-time win and sale may be good in some crazy transactional view; however, if what you seek is a long-term relationship and the advocacy of the client, taking advantage of them and overselling or incorrectly selling them has significant lasting long-term fallout.

You must be able to evaluate every given transaction as to whether there is an appropriate Downselling opportunity to a better product/service (a special, new, improved, discontinued, rebated, or better profit margin item) that will actually serve the client's needs more appropriately.

For example, if a person enters an electronics shop to buy an appliance or entertainment system and is looking at the high-end product, the sales professional may want to avoid making the high-end product sale if they determine that the Customer's exact needs could be met with a less expensive unit. By making the distinction and allowing the buyer to make an informed decision between the two, you do a service to the client and give them significant reason to patronize you in the future.

As another example, when a person wants to join a larger organization (like the military) and you discover that their needs may be better served by another entity within the larger organization, the professional side of you should guide them to that better decision. If you represent the ARMY National Guard and determine a potential recruit's real needs are best served in the NAVY, then refer them to the other organization, rather than your own.

You must recognize appropriate Downselling items, or which products/services you offer that have obvious Downselling opportunities, and role-play some of those as examples with a group. Verbally show them some examples using the Five-Step Selling Process (Claim-Fact/Feature-Benefit-Naildown sequence).

Every Customer contact is an opportunity to meet their needs. If the sales professional does a thorough job in the Inquiry stage of the selling process to uncover their needs (immediate and future), then in the Presentation stage, Downselling options can be presented where appropriate.

Instead of, "this will address your needs", the conversation may be more like, "you may want to consider this instead of that, as this will do the job you require and save you some money…"

You are always looking at the totality of needs that can be fulfilled with the totality of products/services that you represent, all with the best interest of the Customer in mind.

Another example: if you are presenting the purchase of a full-day educational motivational workshop for a conference to a Prospect and you determine that you can satisfactorily deliver what they need in a half-day session, thereby saving them money, make that recommendation and you may find that you have gained a client for life.

You should always be thinking of the best opportunity with every transaction to build a lasting relationship. To make those options available at the time of the initial transaction is the best window of Downselling opportunity.

Downselling can take on many different forms, including a valuable and legitimate reason for continued follow-up with clients, ensuring they are aware of additional ways to enhance their last transaction with you, and thus, build a better and deeper relationship with them. Consider reconnections:

1. As you know the client's needs evolve or change, then you can use new product/service introductions as a reason to stay in contact with new and established Customers and let them know of new offerings, if they would like to make that purchase, upgrade, etc., and if you can work the financials so what they have previously purchased with can be credited in some degree towards their next purchase, even greater respect and leverage.

2. Then use this legitimate re-connection as an opportunity as and when appropriate to solicit referrals from them and their vast network, personally and professionally.

3. Leveraging yourself as a Subject-Matter-Expert and always reflecting on ways to share your unique industry, marketplace opportunities, or perspectives on how to utilize your organization's deliverables more effectively so the client can gain additional ROIs.

4. Leveraging your colleagues as Subject-Matter-Experts and always be reflecting on ways to share their unique industry, marketplace opportunities, or perspectives on how to utilize your organization's deliverables more effectively so the client can gain additional ROIs.

5. Leveraging yourself as a Subject-Matter-Expert and always reflecting on ways to share your data base strategically for introductions within the industry and marketplace opportunities so the client can gain additional ROIs.

6. Use your existing relationship as an opportunity to explore other services or deliverables that you may have that may enhance their professional needs for an upgrade in the relationship or horizontal add-on of other deliverables that you may have.

7. Always be evaluating the marketplace for other suppliers, vendors, manufacturers, etc. that may have a deliverable that can be added or combined to what you have connected to your client on, and by your client acquiring that deliverable it enhances what they have or provide to their subsequent Customers or enhances their marketplace position.

8. Examine the form of the deliverable that you are providing the marketplace and any specific Customer, then evaluate whether you have or could create a new deliverable as an upgrade that enhances what the client is doing with you, and this Down-sale strengthens your relationship and generates additional revenue streams.
    Example: If you are engaged in professional-personal development by attending a human capital development on-site training program and gain value from that experience, this would be the initial sale activity. Then

if there were online learning and development portal self-driven courseware programs and the person you did or are doing business with lets you know about this additional opportunity, as an additional way to increase your skill set and thus marketplace value, you would want to know and consider this, this would be the first follow-up Downselling opportunity.

However, Downselling is about right-selling. So if the client is enthusiastic to purchase quantity items or everything that you have to offer, and that would be over-selling and not appropriate, then Downselling is the right-selling approach. Engage the client as to what the level of appropriate purchase or investment might be, given their ability to use, consume and see a measurable ROI.

You could design regular touchpoints to keep your name in front of the client or marketplace through penning regular, high-value, content-rich articles or an article series/column that can be delivered via social media/internet subscription, (free or for a fee), or via traditional hard copy distribution that reinforce the spirit, theme, reason for the initial client interaction ...

Downselling is about integrity and right-selling.

Another means to fulfilling legitimate Prospect/Customer needs from a Downselling perspective may be to deploy the *Business Integration Grid* ™ (BIG) discussed in Chapter 38. Consider:

1. Connecting your clients and the services or deliverables they need from you with another product or service that a non-competing entity or vendor provides. Now imagine you had forged a referral relationship with those non-competing entities or vendors (partnerships, collaborations, alliance-partners). You could recommend them to serve your clients' needs and generate an additional free revenue stream to you and your organization.

2. Now, explore the same BIG model in reverse, looking at the contacts and Customers that these partners already have relationships with. Brainstorm the massive business development opportunities that may be present and analyze which services or deliverables you have that they would need. Then build a campaign to connect to those contacts and Customers based on your referral relationship with those non-competing entities or vendors. Based off of the relationship you have and the trust factor established with them, and their respective trust factor to their clients, you could now recommend services and deliverables that would serve them in their needs and at the same time generate an additional free revenue stream to you and your organization – and additional revenue streams to those partnered organizations.

Completely fulfilling a Customer's needs with all products/services offered by your organization/department is the responsibility of a professional sales representative and sales leader.

Chapter 38

Performance-Driven Selling©
Business Integration Grid® -
100% of 100% Account
Development & More Business
Opportunities

Great sales professionals have realized that the 80/20 Rule applies to selling – a larger percentage (80'ish percent) of business graduates from a smaller portion of the contact base (20'ish percent). To accelerate your selling opportunities and closing ratios, most selling professionals also overlook the fastest route to more sales from this 20% factor. Recognize the market or areas from which you tend to do the majority of your work and receive the majority of your business from (also known as ones' "Target Rich Environment" (TRE®).

In this application of your TRE, we will focus upon only those Customers that have bought from you or those that you have recruited. To find qualified leads and Prospects that you can immediately engage for faster selling endeavors, start each day by fixating 100-percent of your time first by engaging 100-percent of your Customers on 100-percent of what you have as deliverables to sale. Only until you know you have engaged each of them on what you have to offer and mined them for leads or more business, should you ever entertain finding new unknown leads, suspects and Prospects to talk to.

Typically, in selling, we find a lead and work it into a suspect, and then we engage deeper to determine if that suspect is a qualified Prospect, and if so we engage even deeper to identify their needs and whether we have a solution. If we do, we present that solution and make the case for the sale. And when completed, we start the process over by making the next 'cold' or 'unknown call' into the marketplace. While there is a need for this, it is not the best ROI of time, market connectivity, leveraged relationships, etc. of our time.

Here is what is:

1. Imagine an excel spreadsheet. Across the top are all of the deliverables that you have to offer the marketplace. Whether that is by individual SKU or branded deliverables into grouping or if recruiting someone to your organization, all of the Jobs/MOS/AFSC/Positions/Degrees/Etc..

2. Down the vertical side are all of your contacts that you have established your brand with and have established a trust factor with. Sequentially, start with and include:
    a. All of your (or the organization's) active clients
    b. Followed by all of the inactive clients
    c. Followed by all of the Prospects that were about to graduate to a Customer but stopped for a known or unknown reason
    d. Followed by all of the people that you know, that know what you do, as potential Customers, lead generators or Centers-Of-Influence lead generators and market insight providers.

I refer to this modeling as the Business Integration Grid® and this 100% of 100% focus is quadrant one commitment to the grid (A variation of this model originally created by H. Igor Ansoff and first published in the *Harvard Business Review* in 1957, yet the market today has forgotten its application). To accelerate your selling closing ratios and exceed any selling goal standard, a sales professional should fixate 100 percent of their daily energy first into Quadrant #1 endeavors, then as time allows into quadrant #2, and if any time is remaining on any given day then into quadrant #3. As a selling professional quadrant #4 is best left for off-the selling clock time endeavors.

Deliverables

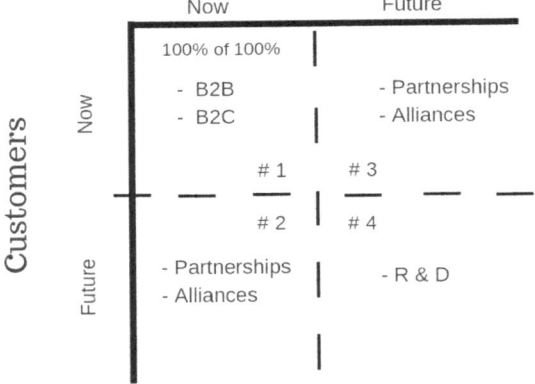

As you administrate your day, manage all of the high impact action items you own, while handling all of the daily unknowns, the strategic focus of quadrant #1 will always yield a greater ROI and it is the single area most selling professionals overlook daily. Consider incorporating into your daily action mix contact endeavors to quadrant #1 contacts, such as (and not limited to):

    1. Regular phone calls follow-up and requests/asks
    2. Regular face-to-face engagements follow-up and requests/asks
    3. Regular email follow-up and requests/asks
    4. Regular social media outreach follow-up and requests/asks
    5. Regular direct mail follow-up and requests/asks

6. Regular texting follow-up and requests/asks
7. Regular personal engagements and follow-up and requests/asks

If you fixate on taking 100-percent care of these contacts first each day, then address all of those that do not know you as viable market options second, you may experience a massive increase in ROI.

Fixate on your 80/20 and drill into that 20-percent factor as your hidden TRE® and identify all of the contacts via the vertical column on your BIG® Model for success.

Refer to Chapter 32 for concentration on how a **100% of 100%** focus can generate greater market growth.

Chapter 39

Performance-Driven Selling©
Cultivating "Advocates &
COIs" From Existing Clients

Great sales professionals don't miss a selling opportunity, nor do they miss an opportunity to network with others to find ways to make others' lives better and easier. By doing so, powerful relationships can be cultivated.

Leveraging and accelerating your selling cycle through engaged relationships with existing clients and converting them to engaged "Advocates" is one of many strategic assets you have in selling. Along with "advocates" you can have other "Centers-of-Influence" that are not always cultivated from the ranks of existing and past Customers/clients.

Examine your professional and personal lives for individuals that believe so powerfully in you and your deliverable(s), that they don't hesitate to talk you up to others. It is these people that can serve as a valuable component in ones' selling world.

Those people that believe so powerfully in You, can be cultivated into "Advocates" – sending business leads to you, recommending you as the solution provider for others challenges and problems. These are the individuals who promote you into the marketplace when you are not available to promote yourself.

"Advocates/Centers-of-Influence" are people that you turn to for advice, suggestions, and counsel. These are strategic people that you can bounce marketing and selling ideas off of. These are the individuals that you can turn to when you have a new product or service available and you want to get the word out. They are well positioned in a marketplace themselves and likely have many people who respect them, that you can cultivate for immediate and future business opportunities. These strategic relationships can serve to be additional minds, eyes, ears and brains in your marketplace and keep calibrated to what is going on 24/7.

"Advocates/Centers-of-Influence" believe strongly in you, trust you, and believe in you both personally and professionally. Therefore, these individuals can serve as a never-ending source of qualified contacts for your Sales Funnel.

Search for "Advocates/Centers-of-Influence" from your most loyal Customers, largest volume Customers, Prospects that sing your praises but for legitimate reasons have not yet become active clients. Look inward to your organization and outward to your social/personal contacts for people that respect and admire you. Look for decision makers in industry, associations, clubs, social organizations, churches, schools (K-18), etc., where you engage others and where there may be opportunities for both sides to gain from one another.

If someone *occasionally* refers business to you or shares insights about what they see happening in the marketplace, do not be mistaken, this is not an "Advocate or Center-of-Influence" – this is merely a person that happened to think about you.

It takes dedicated, sincere, professional continual work to find and maintain an active "Advocate/Center-of-Influence" network. Engage them and treat them like a powerful, qualified lead you want to convert. Consider the *Rule 1-52-X® model* to drip connectivity to monthly and maintain top-of-mind awareness. Strategically embedded "Advocates/Centers-of-Influence" within an organization or Target-Rich-Environment can produce a steady stream of qualified leads and occasional Customers. For an individual to be an "Advocate/Center-of-Influence" they must connect with you on a regular basis – that is the single most important variable to business development and having them serve as a force multiplier for and to you.

Stay connected, send them:

1. Thank you notes or acts
2. New leads for their business
3. Client updates
4. Organizational FYIs, media updates, celebration updates
5. Personal 411 type touchpoints
6. Enroll them into any meaningful, value-added social media and or informational electronic subscription services you offer
7. Etc.

In exploring precise ways to engage your "Advocates/Centers-of-Influence" look at the optics of how you first found them and why they became a Customer. Those two pieces of data will direct you in engaging each "Advocates/Centers-of-Influence" on their own terms and direct you as to how to leverage them for leads in the same sphere from which they came. Example:

1. If a client came to you from an internet search or social media platform, then you have just revealed that there are substantial online analytics that you can use to surf, find, harvest, and follow-up on other virtual leads that may not be calling you.

2. If a client came to you from a social network, club, association, trade organization, institution (for a military Recruiter this could be a specific school), then by

identifying that as a lead source, you can now engage that client for more insights into that sphere.

3. If a client came to you from another existing client, then work your older clients and not just your newest clients for more lead sources from their life touchpoints and always make sure your clients know what has been cultivated, the status of each lead (good or bad), and express sincere appreciation if you want them to remain as an engage "Advocates/Centers-of-Influence."

In order to accelerate your successful selling and market ownership, you must cultivate your "Advocates/Centers-of-Influence," and show them appreciation. You'll know when you have powerful "Advocates/Centers-of-Influence" when these individuals engage you on a regular, meaningful basis.

Chapter 40

Farming Versus Hunting ...
Networking Versus Cold Calling:
The Art & Science to Better
Selling & Lead Flow Management

Cold calling is critical to the lifeblood of any selling organization because it gets your name and deliverable in front of people that a) do not know you exist and that b) are a suited recipient of your solution for their immediate, intermediate and possible long-term needs. You must consistently keep lead flow into your selling pipeline/selling funnel.

We have been raised in a world of hunter-gatherer mentality, and for some this has worked in the immediacy of selling. Big reality check: To sustain immediate sales and long-term sales, a mind-shift must take place with sales professionals and managerial-leaders.

Whether your organization does anything to pull or push leads into the sales pipeline for you and others to follow-up on, you must also perform annual, regular, consistent, lead flow management activities.

Networking is the art-science of farming and cultivating both the immediate relationships that feed immediate selling opportunities while also ensuring continued future feasts. The hunter is the traditional "cold calling" scarcity mentality, and most selling professional's behaviors validate larger volumes of failure and resistance, versus successes and closing rates. Consumers can detect when they are being sold versus when they are being engaged and making a conscious decision to buy.

Whether you are dealing with front-line selling initiatives, inside selling, outside selling or over-seeing selling from a macro strategic focus, the rules of networking engagement apply (B2B, B2C, C2C, C2B). It's all critical in the new world of pedestrian and virtual selling (selling, enlistment, recruitment, membership, etc.). To leverage increased possible new selling endeavors from people that do not know you, leverage all the contacts you have first via leveraged networking, before you fixate on over-coming call reluctance of "cold calling" strangers.

Some essential Networking guide-points:

1. You must have the **Mentality** of being other person centric and truly wanting to understand the other party and assist them in their pursuits – Law of Reciprocity.

2. Getting meaningful, continued, and lasting **Referrals** is also about keeping your eyes open to what you can be doing for others first and continually. Repeatedly legitimate connectivity to clients affords you continued conversational opportunities with them, and this will allow you to recognize touch-points in their life to others that may be beneficiaries of what you have to offer; For example, if you know I am involved in my Home Owners Association then I can link you to neighbors, their family members, the people they work with. Or if you knew I was involved in another area or professional affinity group, then leverage the reach into those networks.

3. Join every appropriate business and personal networking, referral, coaching group in your community

and on-line universe. Ivan Misner, the Founder of the largest and oldest international business lead referral development networking organization, BNI (www.BNI.com) and a regular contributor for years to my www.ProfessionalPerformanceMagazine.com editorial flow, has a time-tested three-step networking model that every professional selling and business owner must live by -**VCP** understanding.

Build **V**isibility in the market first, then ensure you have **C**redibility at all times and in everything you do, then **P**rofitability will come.

1. Understand that **Generational Diversity** impacts how Networking takes place and you must play on the Generational playing field that the other person plays within. So, if someone is social media savvy, you must be as well. If someone is a big face-to-face person, then you must be in their space regularly, etc.

2. Understand that **Gender Diversity** impacts how Networking takes place and you must play on the Gender playing field that the other person plays within.

3. Make sure you do not become desperate and emotional in your presence and remember Networking is both an immediate, intermediate, and long term needs-based endeavor.

4. Apply **Rule 3-3-30®** (a model I learned decades ago when interacting with the late great Bill Tragos, principle of the world's largest advertising firm - TBWA), to your networking. In the first 3-Seconds someone sees you, what does your visual message project? It must captivate them and pull them inward to want more from you. The second 3-Seconds is when the first close face-to-face space is connected. What does your persona project and say about you? The other person has to be able to put into context who you are and

what your broad brand message says. Then, if you have not lost them, the next 30-seconds are the first words that are expressed and exchanged. Here is your message that either pulls them to you or pushes them away from you. What do these words convey about you and are they words that compel the other person to want to engage you further and know more about you?

5. Enroll and be proactive in appropriate **Networking Groups/Associations**. Become involved and committed to Trade, Industry, Peer, Geographic, Referral, and Business clubs, groups, associations. Attend and proactively engage others to PLUS OTHERS first. Look into groups like www.BNI.com, Rotary, United States Junior Chamber/USJaycees, Chamber-of-Commerce business groups that appeal to a specific affinity, etc.).

6. Utilize **Social Media** as a brand builder and awareness resource, it's like planting seeds that others will participate in cultivating with you and that will produce future transformational and transactional outcomes. Look at on-line professional portals for affiliation and regular engagement into – provide value to others first.

7. Track **Your On-Line Analytics**, as another lead source for networking, you should generate a daily report of all the on-line traffic to your website and social-media platforms, from these visitors, pro-actively send a follow-up email to them availing yourself should they have un-met questions needing answers. Something like, *"I noticed you stopped into our website yesterday, thank you, if you have any questions or needs that you did not find answers to, please let me be your personal contact, I can be reached at 111-222-3333 or* xxx@yyy.com*"*

8. **Local Trades**. Subscribe to all industry publications and local business/trade publications that come out and

chronicle what's going on in the business community. These typically provide lists of prospects or updates on movers-and-shakers, or announcements of new business growth expansions and people – all rich sources of smaller lead sources on a weekly to monthly basis as well.

9. **Time and Scheduling Consistency** is critical to lead flow creation through "networking" and "cold calling" endeavors. Talk to the super achievers in your industry or organization (and I mean those people that consistently attain and surpass their selling goal objectives) for best advice as to the days of the week and the times of the day for the best reach out phone calling cycles, IT based campaigns or face-to-face activities.

Stay connected to Everyone. Make sure you maintain a long term big picture focus to return to the Network you have built and continuously are checking in with your contacts (customers, vendors, colleagues, inactive clients, people connected to them, etc.) to see how to be of value to them. Make sure you are a good ambassador and advocate for them by staying on top of their latest endeavors and offerings. Then the Law of Reciprocity will play forward and back to you. Whether that means utilizing your smart technologies to have reminders to reconnect on a daily, weekly, monthly basis with your Network contacts, it takes a lot of energy to build a Network, less to maintain it, and not much to lose it.

With every contact from the above idea lists, always ensure they have your up-to-date contact information in their smart phone directories, copies of your business cards, and any other appropriate connectivity differentiators of value in their possession.

Make utilizing your Network of contacts a regular part of your selling efforts and lead flow contact into your selling pipeline. Remember selling model idea *1-52-X®*, this can be one of those targeted demographics you reach out to once a month or as strategically appropriate.

Evaluating your contacts as networking opportunities, should start your mental juices flowing on even more target rich networking ideas relevant for you, write them down and execute connections into each. Networking should be understood as an essential component of a sales professional and organizations over-all market touch-points. Sustaining long term market presence and selling effectiveness is about the "now" as much as it is about the "future" and far too many people and organizations have a micro "now" mentality and that exhausts everyone in the end.

Chapter 41

Performance Driven Selling©
Orphan-Selling® Can Make
Your Future a Success

One of the greatest strategic selling ideas in your professional selling tool-kit is Orphan-Selling®. When effectively and successfully deployed, it will afford you greater market connectivity than your competition will realize. Orphan-Selling illustrates the habits most selling organizations fall into and illustrates just how lazy most professional selling individuals really are.

Great sales professionals don't miss a selling opportunity, nor do they miss an opportunity left by other short sighted selling professionals in the marketplace. Here is an idea so powerful it is alarming.

I recall a conversation with friends and occasional columnists to my www.ProfessionalPerformanceMagazine.com, Harvey Mackay and Tom Hopkins. The discussion revolved around the amount of lost business growth opportunities that there are for selling professionals if they would remain connected with past clients.

Orphan-Selling® is the strategic concept of adopting the sale that someone else made, and staying professionally connected to them as if they belonged to you all along. This is a universal strategic concept and works whether you are a sales professional, recruiter, client services representative, business development specialist or order taker. Consider:

1. Archive and track every sale you (and your organization) have lost to the competition. Recognize the amount of time and intensity you invested courting that prospect. If they have made a decision to go with your competition, don't get mad, get better. Here is where most selling professionals believe it is time to disconnect from that person, as they believe the selling process is lost and done. You adopt them and stay connected to them as you would if you had sold/recruited them into your organization. Determine when their next buying (next purchase time line or for example in the military when re-enlistment would take place) time line would take place and then by maintaining your adopted relationship as a support agent, go to Subject-Matter-Expert, trusted advisor or agent to their well-being, you would be poised to make the next sale.

Create an excel spreadsheet or run a report from your database of all lost sales in the past 12-months and go backward for the past decade, as appropriate, and now you have a new list of "warm leads" to reconnect to and see about adopting them into your next selling campaign of opportunities.

2. Notice every sales transaction by your competition and record their new customers into your data base as if they were your new customers. If you are a recruiter, then notice the individuals that join your competition as if they were a new member to your organization. If you had built some degree of rapport or relationship with them, don't just walk away from that, stay connected as if you were adopting them into your selling pipeline, and just as you would check-in with your new and existing clients for needs, updates, how you can help them, serve them, and earn their respect, now you can garner business from that relationship.

When it is time for them to buy/enlist again, if they are not satisfied with the organization or agent they previously did business with, you as a professional that adopted them and didn't abandon them, may get the next selling opportunity.

Here is what typically takes place in the selling world: Most new customers once gained are quickly discarded by that organization in terms of after action follow-up, client-care, cultural-connectivity, etc., the energy is for the hunt for the new customer.

Let me get more specific. What you do is "Adopt" the new customers that you lost to someone else, as an "Orphan Account" and treat them as if they had just done business with you. Several things that you can do for these "Orphan Accounts Adopted" to potentially convert them into Centers-of-Influence (COIs) and even potential future "Clients" is to:

1. Immediately send them a Congratulations card for their purchase, affiliation or enlistment with the product/organization they just bought or joined into.

2. Add them to your electronic database system to receive any future (*Rule 1-52-X®; Rule 1-2-3-4-5-X®*) informational items, promotional offers, institutional/trade/industry updates or correspondence that you would send to "your active" prospect pool and client base.

3. Send them future Anniversary cards on the anniversary of their purchase/enlistment for the first three years (or for an enlistment through to their first re-enlistment date as a minimum).

4. Send them, call them or face-to-face facilitate a survey (an Exit Interview of sorts) to understand their buying motives. You could ask three simple survey questions:

(1) "What did you like most about the purchase/enlistment you just engaged into?"

(2) "What do you hope to gain from this decision and why?"

(3) "If there were one thing that you could eliminate from the action, what would that have been or be?" or "Is there anything I did or did not do, that lead you to select the other option for your decision?"

5. Make sure you send them a Personal Contact follow up that if they have a problem with their buying decision, need to talk about their decision, or need a last-minute alternate choice option you would be excited to assist them or share your service/product option with them as a substitute.

6. Selling is hard enough, finding qualified prospects and new clients (customers, new members, clients, soldiers, users, students, buyers of what you have to offer) is the daily challenge for every professional.

Adopting Orphans is another powerful selling behavior that on the front-end may not render any results, but over the long term may generate significant results. By absorbing and adopting those new clients of your competition, you will find that most customers never have contact with the person that sold them once they buy or commit. Never have contact.

Now you become their adopted "Orphan Connection" and many times they will come to see you as their sales professional.

Another way to capitalize on the "Orphan Selling" strategy is to stay in touch with customers even after you have lost them to a competitor. Adopt them and send your follow-up mechanisms to them as if they were still your client. In many cases they may realize that the person they have selected to do business with has abandoned them, and that you care more about them. They'll have buyer's remorse and they may return to you, or send leads to you in the future.

This is a long-term business growth strategy to invest in for lifelong success.

Chapter 42

Performance Driven Selling©
Selling, Advocating & Recruiting
from Your Resume for Accelerated
ROI

Looking to harvest warm and hot lead opportunities? It's the "Acres of Diamonds" that the late great Napoleon Hill wrote about. Leverage your "Resume" as a trajectory accelerator of where to find *Centers-of-Influence* and qualified *Prospective Leads/New Customers* daily. Most business leaders in need of business development ROI, nor selling professionals ever leverage the most powerful asset they have in building their selling portfolio, selling funnel and market share – themselves – their RESUME.

If you don't have a current business narrative or resume, it is time to update or build one. "Resume" your professional adult meaningful life into a memorialized document such as your "Resume" or detailed "LinkedIn' profile. Explore the 360-degrees of connectivity off of every entry and benchmark areas of immediate ROI in your Marketing endeavors, Selling activities, and Administrative undertakings.

What do I mean?

If you do have a resume, then consider updating it. It should be multiple pages in length when you are done with this exercise. Whether you are selling at the board room level or entry level, whether you are B2B, B2C, C2C, P2P or are recruiting a young adult to your organization, it plays the same. Your greatest potential for the greatest meaningful connections, fast track relationships, immediate rapport connections and valuable leads, will come from your "Resume" and not from your interpersonal skills (and yes, they are critical as well) and mere hard work (those are given).

Let's wrap some strategic smart energy around the labor side of what you do to connect in the market place. When you review your "Resume" it will open your eyes to possible demographics (people), organizations (affinity groups and past employers), education and certifications (institutions, programs, courses, on-line platforms, etc. and the people you interacted therein and can add to your developmental network), and new entry points to a marketplace (your associations, volunteer groups, etc.) that you most likely did not recognize before reading this article.

Let your immediate past actions be your benchmark to future reality, what have you really been doing and avoiding?

Look at the architecture of a traditional resume. It will include:

1. *Location* of where you live, and will extrapolate further into every place you have lived from birth to today.

2. *Education* is always a section. Consider not just the highest formal education you have obtained, but where and when. Also consider any *Non-Traditional Education* you have obtained (on-line learning, certifications earned, self-development or self-study), where, when, and in what disciplines.

3. *Employer or work history.* Take each employer entry (as an organizational reference place and the specific jobs you did as task connectors to others) and start examining

those past connections to new people and places to make new connections with. Examine your past life and current life outside of your work, start looking at the analytics of whether you are leveraging those connections for your needs today.

4. *Associations, Volunteer or Extra Curricular* activities may sometimes be listed. Reflect on each as well from the perspective of what, where, when, who.

By using your resume you can make immediate re-connection back to people you have first person connections with (that ideally means you have already established some degree of rapport, trust and credibility with one another.) and you can relate to them more comfortably. This allows them to relate to you on a more meaningful level – now you can make a better 'ask' for what you need as a professional selling person.

Whether I wanted to engage another individual in human capital talent management development endeavors or talk to a young adult about joining the military, the "Resume" is the Key Performance Indicator (KPI) trajectory pathway, or blue-print to what I should be doing.

Example:

1. If I reviewed my resume and noticed other business leaders from outside my primary professional life, then I may start to recognize new lead generators as Centers-of-Influence that I would otherwise have over looked.

2. Or, if I were a Military Recruiter or College Admissions Recruiter looking for places to connect for new or more Centers-of-Influence or new prospects to talk to about how the military could compliment or improve their station in life, then imagine what valuable previously untouched contacts that the resume may shed light upon. If I used to work landscape jobs, I can now walk up to a person working on a maintenance, landscape crew and

engage in a first-person story, no one is above the other and both of you are peer connecting. If I worked in a nursing home doing cleaning, I can have a one-on-one legitimate conversation with anyone in housekeeping or domestic engineering. If I was raised on a farm, I could make a more genuine connection with another agrarian professional. If I went to college on an athletic scholarship I would have a first-person reference with another possible athlete.

A resume guides references you can now place in your marketing or introduction letters, emails, social media campaigns, into your presentations and conversations to make you have a relational connection to others.

If I am not in a direct selling or recruiting capacity, I too have an obligation to generate LEADS for my organization, in an attempt to keep it thriving. I can use these same guide-posts to find great new leads that others may not have access to or know about, and from those leads I can personally direct them to the selling or recruiting colleagues for even greater ROI.

Use your resume to guide where you should be and eliminate selling resistance today and generate greater RPI today.

Chapter 43

Performance Driven Selling©
Selling to Mission Statement
& Personal Position Statements

Y ears ago, I was attempting (unsuccessfully) to get in the door to make a presentation to a Fortune 500 Firm. Then one day, I realized that when selling to an individual (B2C or C2C) you must position yourself and your offer to be "other person centric" and serve their needs, ideally, their immediate needs. The same holds true when selling to a business (C2B or B2B).

One powerful way to determine if you are pushing jello up-hill or have a directed means of serving a business is to review their website, annual report, on-line or traditional promotional literature, their websites and find their Mission Statement. A Mission Statement serves as an organizations map (just as knowing an individual's Personal Position Statement) and is supposed to serve as their GPS system of sorts from which all their decisions and actions are benched marked off of before implementing. By reading their Mission Statement you can determine how to elicit their emotional and logical attention towards what your deliverables may be and how you can position your consultative questions and discussion to determine how best to serve them. Consider:

1. When selling to organizations, identify what their *MISSION STATEMENT* says; This will be driven by what their value system is and is not ...

2. When selling to an individual (or attempting to Recruit an individual to your organization or cause) identify what their *PERSONAL POSITION STATEMENT* says; This will be driven by what their value system is and is not ...

Knowing this STATEMENT will greatly accelerate your next actions to success or disconnection.

By using their pre-determined trigger values, beliefs, goals, objectives, psychological drivers and words in your presentation and responses, you can elicit a higher level of interest and serious consideration of your offer. Look for:

1. What specific "call to action" statements are listed?

2. What do they say are their "fundamental reasons" for being in business or having the identity they state to hold and how can you attach yourself or your deliverables (Features/Benefits) to that claim in a way that they can see you as an ally in their pursuits?

3. Do any of their words indicate or provide any clues as to their immediate, intermediate, and long term "goals or purposes"?

4. Who do they indicate they seek as "ideal partners" in their business relationships?

5. Who do they indicate they "see themselves as" and how do you then position yourself, your deliverables, your clients so they see a positive effect in associating with you?

Once you internalize their *Mission Statement/Personal Position Statement* as an organization (or in selling to an individual identifying what their Personal Positional Statement would be), then in your presentation (word doc, email, PowerPoint, conversation, demonstrations, tours, etc.) copy paste their own words as lead in statements to what you want to discuss with them or present to them, and use their words in your dialogue to further personalization your interaction. In essence use their words as the set-up to your offer as the solution.

Selling to Mission Statements/Personal Position Statement

Fine tuning your presentation to the prospect or clients real core needs can be done by becoming familiar with their *Mission Statement/Personal Position Statement*.

Read the sign hanging on the wall in their lobby as you wait to make your presentation, or review their website, or their Annual Report. Maybe it is even on their business card or literature. Whether their Value Statements drives their *Mission Statement/Personal Position Statement* or their *Mission Statement/Personal Position Statement* drives their operating Values, you can look for areas where you can assist them to really drive their point home. In selling to an individual determine what their true motivators are and who they see themselves to be, this will serve as their personal *Mission Statement/Personal Position Statement*.

Most *Mission Statement/Personal Position Statement* will identify six selling opportunities. As you examine a prospect's *Mission Statement/Personal Position Statement* to make your initial presentation to or review an existing client's *Mission Statement/Personal Position Statement* to determine additional follow up selling opportunities (up-sale, cross-sale, add-on selling), you will want to:

1.   Identify what each sentence really commits to

2. Determine how to use their exact language in your written proposal or verbal presentation

The six critical elements to a sound *Mission Statement/Personal Position Statement* structure will be:

1. **Who** – should be identified as to who owns or is committing to what
2. **What** – is being sought or committed to and thus valued above all else
3. **When** – actions and behaviors are to be demonstrated and in what order of commitment
4. **Where** – identifies the geography of the commitments and in chronological order of importance
5. **Why** – will be the driving or compelling force behind the commitments and will identify the rationalization and motivation behind their sense of being
6. **How** – demonstrates the manner in which they commit to their actions, what they may deem as legal, ethical, cost effective in the driving forces

Once you illuminate these answers from your prospect or clients' perspective, you can benchmark your entire presentation against what they spell out as important. You can even use it as reference markers in either your print campaign or verbal presentations. You can reference one of their key statements and then transition into one of the ways you can address that. And then continue onward throughout your presentation in a systematic manner to the closing step of the selling process.

This same model obviously applies when selling to an individual as well, but by now you have already made that mental leap of understanding. If you are selling your service/product to an individual (or are working to recruit them to your endeavor or cause) you would look for evidence of their past actions to determine what is really important to them, not others, and then make the connection from those past commitments and accomplishments and how you can aid them in furthering that ambition to make your sale.

Where to go for insights for connectivity:

1. Annual Reports
2. Owner, Chairman or CEO Reports to share holders
3. Websites
4. Trade Journals and Associations that a point-of-contact may be affiliated with
5. Social Media sites that the point-of-contact may participate in and have posting on
6. Other clients or contacts you have that may also have connectivity with new targeted point-of-contact
7. Etc.

Mission Statement/Personal Position Statements serve as the maps by which people operate and by which people look to make decisions off of. When you can aid others in doing precisely that, they will typically embrace your offer.

Chapter 44

Performance Driven Selling©
Leveraging Social Media &
Viral Marketing in Selling &
Lead Generation as a Sales
Professional, Association Membership
or Military Recruiter –
it's all the same rule book.

Connecting where your market really lives is critical to keeping your name, brand and offer top-of-mind in the prospect pool and with your current client base. Making sure your name is where the market is, is a critical factor to success.

McDonalds and Marriott taught the World decades ago that one major and compelling factor to marketing and positioning is – location-location-location. Today, companies like Facebook, Yahoo, Pinterest, Amazon, and Zappos teach us that "location" can refer the space you occupy in the social media world of your market?

How do you keep 'YOU' relevant for that market, *and most importantly once done, how do you leverage that for lead generation connectivity and more business – this is the new force multiplier for account development and your portfolio expansion.*

Whether you are positioned as a B2B, B2C, C2C or hybrid of something in the middle, applying social media into your arsenal of ways to reach the market and stay connected to the market is the new normal.

Think of social media as another channel in the media, communication, connectivity arsenal. Your ability to integrate all of these as appropriate and when appropriate, provides you with a market advantage.

Successful selling professionals across a myriad of industries, as well as educational and military recruiters that I have coached for decades, have recognized that while many of the traditional platforms of marketing, canvassing, calling and selling remain the same (and are critical), some of the distribution channels for reaching the market have changed, evolved, and if embraced can increase your over-all effectiveness substantially. You can reach more, faster, directly and with little to no revenue involved.

While an organization can have dedicated personnel and assets to this new social media space and viral marketing channels, it is also incumbent upon the actual selling professional to occupy this space on an even greater micro level, be more organic, and make it fit your personality and leverage your advocates (Centers-of-Influence) to become viral.

The relevant messaging and push/pull marketing TouchPoints™ are actually endless and while this can be an undertaking that is little additional effort on your behalf, it can become your greatest selling point, branding play, lead generation channel, and greatest way to reach mass market with no additional revenue funding.

Generation Millennial and Z may be aware of the traditional old world rules are relevant still, there are new rules for engaging the mind-share and movement of markets as well – social media platforms and accelerated connectivity that are their centers of gravity.

Whatever the social media platform is that your market is engaged with, that is the social media market for consideration.

Be mindful that Social Media is great at brand building, brand awareness, and building a following, but seldom does Social Media translate into immediate sales transactions, so you must remain focused on the complete selling process.

Explore these ideas and allow your own creative juices to flow and reveal even more powerful strategies and tactics for making your mark on the market place.

Consider these strategic and tactical actions daily:

1. Connect your **Facebook** account (Your Page or a Fan Page), with your **LinkedIn** account, with your **Twitter** account (and any other social media account that your prospects live within and that your advocates are addicted to), so when you send a brief "action oriented" message or update to one account it replicates across every account simultaneously.

2. Connect your **Website Home Page** account, with your **Facebook, LinkedIn, Twitter (and other relevant social media platforms)** account, so when you make informational, promotional, awareness updates to your website it replicates across your social media platforms and unique followers. And reverse, as you post to any one of the other social media platforms it reverse replicates on your home website page(s) accordingly and appropriately. This allows you to leverage the social media platform power and increase you reach into larger on-line communities. If you for example retweet a message it populates onto and across your platforms.

3. It takes at least seven relevant social media messages, alerts, updates to capture a person's attention.

4. Anytime you are meeting with a high-profile contact that would have leverage on others you are attempting to attract, *Tweet* that.
   a. Utilize instant communication platforms to inform your market and potential prospects where you are, when you will be somewhere
   b. As you are meeting for example at a trade show/informational booth or table, at a job fair, college fair, business networking event, etc., you could send continuous updates out thereby letting others know to come by and see you or join in on the fun you are having
   c. If you will be meeting with new customers or influential others (COIs), have then duplicate your efforts and push Tweets of other social media platform messaging connectivity to their followers about you and to stop by
   d. If you just made a great sale, share that as a 411 with your platforms, this can create buzz and energy for others to want to have the same experience with you

5. Allow people to join you when you may be meeting socially with others, make this a conversational community.

6. If you are at an event where there is signage or something visually that can spread your message without you having to type or say it, shoot a picture and post that to your *Facebook* page, *Tweet* it, *Snapchat* it, *Instagram* it, *Pinterest* it, post on your own *Website*, *etc.*

   a. In the picture *'tag'* and identify everything within the pic that can have magnetic appeal with others in the social media search world

7. If you are at an event where there is signage or something visually that can spread your message without you having to type or say it, shoot a picture and send to your advocates, followers and leverage onto the 'hosts' social media platforms by strategically '**hashtagging**' their name, brand, key personalities.
   a. In the picture 'tag' and identify everything within the pic that can have magnetic appeal with others in the social media search world

8. If you have just had a selling victory, share that through the words of the customer to your *Facebook* page, *Tweet* it, *Snapchat* it, *Instagram* it, *Pinterest* it, add it to your own *Website, etc.*

9. Every time you make a selling transaction happen, share it and have the customer (new customer using your product, new member that joins your organization, you have just enlisted someone into your Service, etc.) do the same to their social media space (it is about mass expansion to your market space and more importantly the other persons' market space of followers and contacts.).

10. Here is where the power of social media can generate instant leads for you and where you can find your next sale. Follow the *LIKES* for instant lead generation and leverage this smartly.

11. Every time you make a sale or enlist someone into your organization, shoot a picture of them with you (you are the representing agent and thus market product that must be recognized.) and have them post it to their social media platform
    a. Then for several days after this sale/enlistment follow that person's social media platform posting, stop-in to their social media platforms home page where they posted your picture and monitor who has "Liked" their photo,

b. Click on that Like and go to that new contacts social media platform and do a cursory review to determine if they look like a Prospect, and if so, click back out and onto the original social media platform page of your customer, and click a message (or text them or call them.) and have your new client-customer arrange a three-way meeting ASAP with the new Prospect. Leverage your new customer/enlistment to assist you in making your next sale.

c. Accelerate your social media lead generation by doing the same with your competition. Regularly review their social media platforms, if you know your direct selling agent competitor, monitor their social media platforms. look at their social media platforms for new posting of clients-customers, go their new customers' personal social media platforms and see what their followers may reveal to you for lead generation. Then do the same here as Point "a" and "b" above.

12. 80% of sales are closed/made on the fifth contact or beyond, so allow social media to compliment your Touch-Points and accelerate the mind-share you own.

13. Critical to why most selling professionals are really mere order takers and accept whatever the market will provide, 48% of sales people never follow up or don't follow up in a timely manner to have any positive impact on the initial contact activity.

14. My research with the largest sales forces in the Nation over the past twenty years (Pfizer Pharmaceutical, ARMY National Guard, IBM, Anheuser-Busch, ABM, and more) is that 12% of sales people only make two to three contacts and stop; 25% of sales people make a second contact and stop; Less than 10% of sales people make more than three contacts with a prospect or lead.

15. Another reason most selling professionals never reach apex success, is that 70% of sales people have and use no systems on a regular basis to manage their book of business. Make your social media a systematic part of your daily efforts – Coffee and Tweet to start the day.

16. If your organization is fortunate enough to have in-house or out-sourced Communications/PR/ Marketing/Public-Affairs/Social Media Marketing/Etc. individuals, teams, departments, or agencies connected to you, then it is critical that all parties work together whenever possible and synergistically leverage what one another is doing with same hash tags and links, and do so across all appropriate social media platforms.

17. Ideas of meaningful communication:
    a. Any new service offer or product offer you have, you should build a social media announcement or blitz around other traditional announcement/marketing campaigns
    b. Any new customer endorsement, testimonial, or affirmation can be communicated
    c. Celebrating another person's accomplishments, accolades, awards, notations can be communicated
    d. Any urgent call-to-actions; any celebrity engagements for your industry, business, space should be communicated
    e. Have a regular communication update or blog or bulletin board of posts or re-posts from individuals within your organization with exciting messages that your prospects and advocates could become addicted to following
    f. You could spread around the content development for posts by assigning a regular brief from key constituents within your organization, so the message is not always coming from you

g. The ideas are endless, so let the creative DNA flow.

If you are not proactive in this space, your competition will be and they will make the sales you miss. Not because they have a better value proposition, but because the market can't find you, does not see you, or can't easily access your services.

Keep in mind that once acknowledged that the social media space was a place for Generational X/Y and Millennials to hang-out within, today the reality is if you do business with Generation Z, this is their norm address. And some research is even revealing that a ghost demographic and possible new explosion in traffic is actually with the Baby Boomer Generation – so if you have prospects and customers here or even influencers here now you have a means to reach their mindshare.

Once widely accepted that on-line internet traffic and website access was through traditional computers, social media today is an on-the-go instant connectivity reality via a range of virtual mobile devices. And these devices while not always accessible for live phone conversations, can be used in signal (text/picture) transmission 24/7.

If you want to know how to connect with your market and what messages grab their attention, simply watch, observe, and ask. Play where the market is. Better yet, predict where the market is evolving and be there when they arrive.

Chapter 45

Performance-Driven Selling©
Staying Connected to Your
Leads, Prospects & Customer-To-Be
with Follow-Up Rule 1-2-3-4-5-X®
or System 1-2-3-4-5-X®

There are a few reasons why most sales professionals do not generate the level of business or sustained business they could. One of those, is poor to no follow-up system and discipline. It is easy to become so engaged in daily activities, processing what one believes to be the holy grail of their next sell or digging deep into their next administrative task, that engaging potential customers, building relationships, and facilitating transactions have been neglected.

Research by subject matter experts presented in professional publications such as, *Professional Selling Power Magazine* and *www.ProfessionalPerformanceMagazine.com* consistently reveals that most selling individuals give up after the third to fourth attempt at follow-up. Unfortunately, most sales take place after the 5th or Xth contact. In order to succeed, you must know what your number "X" is and create a system to stay connected until then.

This system must become a part of your operational DNA, whether you automate this process or maintain it personally and manually.

Here is one that has served me well for years. I have advocated this to clients for decades and when it is applied, once inactive contacts have been brought back to life.

And yes, before your negative internal voice kicks in, you can utilize technology to aid you and you can adjust it as appropriate, but here is the general rule of methodology. Have a system (any customer contact data base will work) that allows you to track every contact you make. Have all of the tracking fields necessary to enable you to track, explore trends, and search by needs. Have an endless "Note Field" within each contact profile entry for additional notes, copy-paste of texts and emails, etc., so you are always in the know. Then deploy this Model as a system and hard fast Rule for operation on only those contacts you deem as "hot leads".

Model 1-2-3-4-5-X for Consistent Follow-Up and Follow-Through Self-Management:

1. *1 = First Touch-Point = First day:* Within the first 24-hours of getting or meeting a contact, you must (1) Call them, (2) Text them, (3) Email them, or (4) Go See them to determine the next progression/action. If you are unable to reach them, push that name forward for follow-up 48-hours (2-days) later.

2. *2 = Second Touch-Point = Two days Later:* If no contact is made within that first 24-hours, then move that contact forward in your Outlook, Database, Calendar or Manual Call Report system (etc.) to re-connect 48-hours (2-days later) later. Also drop a hand-written note in the mail to them at this time point with a Call-To-Action comment and a second business card, this will have just arrived by your next/third touch-point.

3. *3 = Third Touch-Point = Three days later:* If no contact is made within the first 72-hours, then move that contact forward in your Outlook, Data Base, Calendar or Manual Call Report system (etc.) to re-connect 72-hours

later (3-days later), this would push the Prospect Name from time of original connection (Day One) now at three touch-points spaced out over a seven day period.

4. *4 = Fourth Touch-point =One Week Later/Out:* If no contact is made within this first 6-7 day window, then move that contact forward in your calendar system to re-connect one week out from this third touch-point. If there was a legitimate reason for you to follow-up and connect with them at step #1 of the 1-2-3-4-5-X system, and they have not responded asking you not to contact them, continue to follow up.

5. *5 = Fifth Touch-point = One Month Out:* If no contact is made within this next time sequence, push the lead out five more business days, then again move that contact forward in your calendar to re-connect one week out from this third touch-point. If there was a legitimate reason for you to follow-up and connect with them at step #1 of the 1-2-3-4-5-X system, and they have not responded asking you not to contact them, continue to follow up.

6. *X = X Touch-point = Once Month Out:* If no contact is made within follow-up "CONTACT 1-2-3-4-5-X Model" then push that contact into your follow-up system for a once monthly follow-up or what forward day sequence is appropriate for you, until you can qualify their status. The follow-up touch-point could be done via (1) Call them, (2) Text them, (3) Email them, or (4) Go See them to determine the next progression action. You may want to enroll them into to any electronic system that automatically sends any value based non-selling message (content rich blog, articles, white papers, newsletters, digital magazine or digital books, etc.) to them as well. Ask your network if they can provide any intel on this contact and assist you in connecting.

You can adjust the X-Touchpoint for the rotation that is appropriate for your business and the hot lead you are working. Maybe you re-loop and begin at 1-2-3-4-5 again; Or, the X-Touchpoint could be every ten days; Etc.

For the past two decades, I have found measurable ROI from consistently adding and reaching out to new contacts in my system, and then using that system as a hard and fast Rule. My teams and clients report significant growth opportunities when they are diligent in using a structured follow-up and follow-through system.

Remember, most sales professionals will attempt to reach a contact 1-4 times before deeming it a bad lead and giving up. However, research always illustrates that most sales take place after the 5, 6 or 7th attempt to connect.

As long as the contact stays "hot lead" status and you have no data to downgrade that lead, then explore all of the different touch-points in your arsenal:

1. Call them
2. Text them
3. Email them
4. Use social media platforms to message them. (There are multiple touch-point options here)
5. Reconnect with the source that gave you the lead and ask them to assist you in reaching them
6. Mail them
7. Special delivery them (FedEx, UPS, local Courier Service, etc.)
8. Go see them

Whatever you do, don't give up. Research reflects that over use of any one touch-point communication connection, can cause someone to want to opt-out with you. But, using a rotation and combination of touch-points as you feel comfortable, is seen as different connectivity points, and very few will see you as over-reach.

To accelerate your effectiveness at maintaining market share, market intelligence, and market leverage opportunities you should deploy this model or system with your Top Centers-Of-Influences (COIs) and Top Customers (albeit a shorter more manageable list) as well.

Chapter 46

Performance Driven Selling©
Three Keys to Follow Up Success

Have you heard the saying "The early (smart) bird catches the worm?" The same goes for the smart sales professional with the best professional follow-up.

The opportunity to make a sale is a special event and when a prospect requests more information for a possible additional sell, your follow-up can make or break the deal.

In my decades of selling I have noticed that most sales professionals make the Sale many times. Yet, because they do not know how to read the buying acceptance clues and SHUT UP, they keep talking and un-sell the prospect.

Studies indicate that follow-up alone can significantly increase a sales professional's closing ratio and business volume. Yet most sales professionals don't take advantage of the opportunity.

Few sales are actually made from contact-to-contract in one easy, efficient, expedited manner. Sometimes they do and the importance of studying that flow for replication is critical and a success trait of super achievers. However, most selling transactions must go through a chronological flow in the mind of the recipient and require follow-up well beyond the 4th interaction.

There are three ways in which a sales professional can chose to follow-up with prospects. They are:

1. Visual

2. Auditory

3. Kinesthetic (interactive/face-to-face)

Time of follow-up is critical. Too soon may appear over-bearing and too late may seem like an after-thought that lacks sincerity.

There are a lot of ways to keep your name and message in front of prospects and customers including:

VISUAL -

1. personal note card with your name on it

2. email gram

3. appropriate social media connections

4. fax follow-up note, reminder, FYI

5. special "Thank You" gift/offering

6. an article clipping of relevant interest

7. social media platforms

8. texting

AUDITORY -

1. personal voice mail message

2. follow-up telephone call

3. recorded gift offering

4. appropriate social media deliverable

5. social media platforms

KINESTHETIC -

1. personal follow-up by sales professional or field representative

2. invitation offering to an event/pre-event

4. appropriate social media deliverable

5. leveraging a Client or COI on your behalf to reach out to the prospect

In order to have maximum impact, any action must be taken in a timely manner and it must be relevant for that prospect or customer.

Remember: The early sales professional gets the sale and gets the repeat sale.

Chapter 47

Performance Driven Selling: Let the NIGHT SHIFT Be Your GPS to More Business Opportunities

Imagine looking at your market differently and realizing that it has always existed, yet you never tapped into it. It's like a manufacturer having one shift and exploring expanding to a second physical site, while completely over-looking expanding to a second or a third shift within its present physical capacities first.

Most selling and recruiting professionals look at their market place through the lens of how they work that marketplace. If you work traditional hours of 7 AM to 5 PM, then you look at the market of opportunities through that same lens. If you have been conditioned to work even fewer hours, then the chances of you being successful are greatly diminished.

You must learn what truly works for lead generation and marketplace engagement strategies and then apply those strategies rather than leaning on old, unsuccessful behaviors.

If you want to explode your market share, start operating from a **"Market-Potential"** perspective. "Market-Share" is what percentage of the existing buying/joining business pie you own versus the competition. "Market-Potential" is uncovering new markets no one is working, and folding this into your strategic Sales Business Plans (SBP) and daily actions.

Where is this mysterious potential market you are missing? It is in the exact same zip codes or markets that you are already working.

It's all about the *NIGHT-SHIFT* mentality or an out-of-the-box mentality to business development. Over the past 30 years, 99.9% of selling professionals and sales management that I have interacted with evaluate the market from a traditional lens of 7 AM to 5 PM or a "Traditional Day-Shift" mentality.

Super achievers think 24/7 (most people operate in roughly 16-hour a day cycles from awake to sleep time frames, as that is when they are awake and operational). To find greater COIs, Advocates, Prospects, Customers, Lost Customers, or colleagues that you may otherwise never or seldom interacted with, think about where the people and opportunities are. The *NIGHT-SHIFT Mentality* becomes activated and your Mental GPS will see all of the low hanging fruit opportunities that you can immediately leverage yourself into.

If you need to get into a closed market, open a new market, or find new low hanging fruit, it may be right there in the same zip codes, databases, neighborhoods that you have already been traveling within. It's just not during the hours you've been traveling.

Evaluate what you market and have to sell. Consider as an example:

1. If I were selling on-line learning and development there is an endless and untapped list of demographics that I may not ever see. Now, if I start evaluating the market through the lens of 5 PM to 7 AM, I may be able to identify a new market of "Potentials".

2. What if I were a military Recruiter or more specifically a Recruiter in the National Guard? If I begin evaluating the market through the lens of 5 PM to 7 AM rather than the traditional day-shift mentality, I can identify who is working, where they are working, where they take their breaks or lunches, and who may already be employed and pre-vetted because of their employment. My organization could benefit from these individuals and they could benefit from our organization

Maybe I should call this *NIGHT-SHIFT* marketplace your unseen parallel universe of opportunities. Go forth and ensure the *NIGHT-SHIFT knows about you.*

Chapter 48

Performance Driven Selling©
Using Other Forms of
Technology to Compliment
Your Sales Effectiveness

Just because you can, does not mean you should. And just because you don't know, does not mean you don't need to know – and use when appropriate.

When used effectively and appropriately, technology in your sales presentation and follow-up can be an accelerator to success. When misused or overused, it can become a hindrance. Understanding the new and evolving technologies and how to use them in the daily selling world is a primary responsibility of the sales trainer, sales manager and business owner.

Technology is evolving at such a fast pace that whatever technology plan one develops may be outdated by the time it's implemented. Your ability and willingness to be flexible is critical to implementation and success.

Think of it this way, "Technology" can be:

1. A sales professional equipped with a portable data instrument that allows for access to a database (CRM)

and the knowledge of how to leverage your database efficiently in real-time.

2. Instant communication, updates, announcements, grams, newsletters, etc., through access to ones' e-mail addresses. You can reinforce your prospecting or early stage relationship building endeavors with contacts, by making strategic connections at a new level before-during-after an initial contact or presentation.

3. Communication, advertisement, awareness, order entry, registration and subscriptions via an organizations website presence or QR like (or evolved) code and scan.

4. Laptop computers, portable printers, hard copy faxes or eFaxes, email capabilities and cellular phones can enable a sales professional to telecommute and have a virtual office where ever they are in the world.

5. Teleconferencing, video-conferencing, satellite connections, high speed digital access and connections allows for audio and video interaction from remote locations.

6. Texting (instead of calling) to transfer information or reinforce connections.

7. You can load informational and promotional information and items into cloud platforms and provide individuals or groups with a simple pass code to gain additional information or premium value-added touch-points. In return, you gain additional text/cell number registers and have another source of free instant connectivity to prospects or customers.

8. Use analytics (i.e. Google analytics) or your website domain mastery to track ISP address and visitors to your websites in real-time and automate instant follow-up responders to grab their attention and offer reach-back

connectivity to that unknown visitor. This data is rarely known or collected by selling organizations and opportunities to make sales are lost.

9. Use social media platforms to reinforce your brand and messaging, and to connect with key prospects, customers and the marketplace.

10. Make sure your 21st Century store-front, your website, is user friendly and is easy and inviting for the customers to find, enter, experience, and take action.

11. Benchmark off of your competition or analyze the last lost hot prospect you were working. Analyze the touch-points that took place between them and your competitor so you can strategize against or elevate the game and best them next time.

With the availability of differing technology in the professional sales persons world, the question is, "How does one compliment their selling efforts with technology?"

For example: You can keep a potential buyer informed of additional feature updates to a proposal via email. This is non-threatening as no one would actually be talking live to one another.

Or, modify *Rule 1-52-X*™ to have multiple ways to connect with the market, as opposed to just using two to three touch-points. See technology as a selling partner to be embraced and used effectively.

Consider how you can incorporate technology to make a greater impact with the prospect or client, and in many instances the influencers around them.

Chapter 49

Performance Driven Selling©
Time Management Effectiveness
with The "Quadrant Manager" System:
Increase Your Productivity by
A Factor of Four

Being "active" and being "productive" are worlds apart. Many sales professionals have a lot of activity going on around them, yet when the daily dust settles they seem to generate less bottom line results than others. Being "active" is not the same as being "productive".

Sales professionals must understand that managing time and having the self-discipline to stay focused, is crucial to maximizing every precious moment for prospecting, customer contact, selling, marketing and taking care of administrative responsibilities.

To maximize time, you must understand the concept of Primetime for Primetime endeavors. Start by asking three strategic questions to determine what activities need to be scheduled at what time intervals each day. Consider:

1. As a sales professional, do you have your greatest over all daily energy in the AM or PM hours?
2. Within that window of time (If you're an AM than that would be from whatever time your day starts through Noon or if you're a PM person that would be from Noon

through the typical hour you end each day), define the hours that constitute that AM or PM notation.

3. Now within those hours, when are you at your "peak performance?" This is ones' "Primetime".

For example: A person may have Primetime or peak performance hours from 6 AM through 9 AM. These are the hours with the least amount of distractions and fewest gatekeepers between them and targeted prospects/customers.

Sales professionals must recognize the greatest level of "productivity" occurs when only high level important items take place within the "peak performance-primetime" times

The "Quadrant Manager System™" allows for a universal overview to ones' work to be seen, planned and monitored. Most sales professionals have had days where a lot of things got done or a lot of people were called and even days were a lot of people were seen or a lot of materials written/completed, but at the end of the day, they realized they had overlooked another important area.

The "Quadrant Manager System" allows for work to be managed from an aspect of not what one would like to get done. but more so from an aspect of what is important and must be done. Also, the system is powerful as it keeps all important work areas moving forward at the same time.

To use the "Quadrant Manager System™" there are three steps.

First Step: Create the template that you will write into (do so on a blank piece of paper, modify the template and add it into ones' day planner, etc.). To do so, simply draw a large "plus sign".

Second Step: Place entries into the template. Log or write down a maximum of three entries per category. This allows you to perform a fast, mental exercise of all the items that you could assign to their according quadrant, if you could only have three items per each quadrant, then what are the most impactful, ROI - producing? Here you just write down up to (and never more than) three entries per quadrant. You do not need to prioritize just yet.

Third Step: Now, review one quadrant at a time.. Look at each quadrant's tasks and prioritize them. Place a "1" beside the most important item in each of the four quadrants. Then move on to #2 and a #3 in each quadrant.

The instrument can look like this:

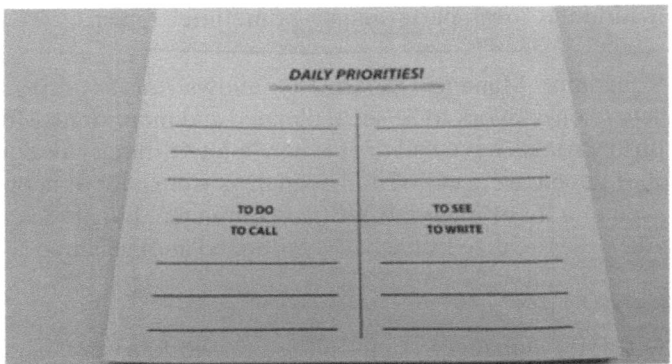

The "Quadrant Manager System" is a more efficient tool for managing overall work responsibilities which allows sales professionals to gage when they are focusing on low priority items, are off track, or are avoiding work.

Another powerful way to use the "Quadrant Manager System" to enhance selling effectiveness, is to develop two additional and more specific "Quadrant Managers" for execution on a daily and weekly basis. Imagine the typical selling funnel or selling pipeline diagrams, you could have:

1. A **"Marketing-Quadrant Manager System"** that would outline the top three "To Dos', To Calls', To Sees' and To Writes'" that can feed the Sales Funnel

from a marketing and prospecting basis and lead to future selling opportunity contacts on a *weekly basis.*

2. **Develop a "Sales-Quadrant Manager System"** that would outline the top three "To Dos', To Calls', To Sees' and To Writes'" that can immediately move you to a Close in the selling process on a *daily basis.*

Sales professionals must also think in specific terms of "marketing" and "selling" time responsibilities. The "Quadrant Manager System" powerfully addresses all three areas of responsibility.

Chapter 50

Performance Driven Selling©
Using A Contact Database
Management System To Assist
in Your Sales Efforts

Effective account management and development will make or break the sales professionals' performance cycle, selling funnel or pipeline and their ability to understand their market, and own their marketplace.

Attempting to stay mentally aware of every account, key prospect, suspect, COIs and influence-makers status and next call-to-action with them is just not possible. However, an electronic account database system (customer relationship management software) empowers you to greater levels of connectivity.

There are a wide range of software options and vendor partnership possibilities, so selecting your system for your computer hardware is important. Some of the leading options are:

1. Antraport
2. FileMaker Pro
3. GoldMine
4. ACT
5. Excel (custom built system)
6. Internal organic systems

7. InfusionSoft
8. HubSpot
9. Etc.

No matter what system you choose, you must take the time to understand it and utilize it most effectively now, and learn how to modify it later (and with limited to no additional costs) as you grow. I use the extensive annotated Note Section I to create my own Note Key words or Coding system for internal searches that the existing system does not already allow.

The database system that you use should allow you to store the following data points and therefore do searches accordingly. The database "template" should be able to do:

1. **Register a "date-field"** for follow-up or call back, so that on that specific date your computer brings up an automatic call report of individuals to be contacted.

2. **"Code" in each entry individually based on their level of importance**. Code numbers of 1 through 4 as an example. Make your codes easy, the more complex you make the codes does not actually result in greater ROI in selling – simple wins.

3. **Store personal contact data**
   a. personal name
   b. address
   c. city
   d. state
   e. zip
   f. phone
   g. cell phone
   h. email
   i. alternate telephones
   j. expandable notes section
   k. social media platforms as appropriate

4. Store professional contact data

    a. organizational name
    b. title
    c. address
    d. city
    e. state
    f. zip
    g. phone land base and cell phone
    h. fax
    i. email
    j. alternate telephones
    k. expandable notes section
    l. social media platforms as appropriate
    m. website(s)

The "date-field" is important. When an account asks to be contacted on a specific date, you can log this into the "date-field" section. Then when the computer is booted-up on that date, a ready prepared list of contacts is made available to the sales professional for immediate action. This creates all future call back lists.

The client "code" section is also valuable, by placing a code value to every entry, a sales professional can do a database search at any time to determine the number of qualified contacts in any specific category. The "code" is also valuable in performing category specific direct mailings, email promotions, fax marketing campaigns to suspects, prospects or active clients. Below is the "coding" system that I have used in the professional services industry (as a performance Coach-Consultant-Trainer-Speaker).

Code 1 = a contact that has MONEY, NEED, DATE for acquisition of your offer.

Code 2 = a contact that meets two of the above three criteria.

Code 3 = a contact that meets one of the above three criteria.

Code 4 = doesn't meet any of the above three criteria, yet earns a position within the database (i.e., they might be a person of influence over a criteria Code 1, 2 or 3 contact name: a family member or friend; someone who may not be a buying customer but serves a marketing or promotional purpose).

This sort of a system allows me to manage my extensive database and do strategic account and database analysis which then drives my marketing, selling, etc. work to generate business and gain greater market awareness.

If the system that you use allows for easy modifications or additional data entry sections to be added as your business grows or changes, even better. If you can execute software activities from within the database, thus saving you time, this is even more effective. For example, if you can pull names or contact data and create and send email campaigns or direct mail campaigns, brilliant. If you can automatically set follow-up automated touch-points, even better. Let your creative juices flow for relevant ways and reasons to stay connected to your database.

With your database, you can now become more effective at understanding and using the analytics on your dashboard, understanding how big data can help you to manage your market:

1. You will be able to quickly scan your data base by Codes and Dates as a daily routine to ensure you are on top of everything that matters.

2. You will be able to perform your own reconnaissance and recognize where hidden opportunities lay, and where you may be dropping balls.

3. You will be able to make yourself look more strategic and bigger in your marketplace by being able to deploy much more effectively, thoroughly and consistently strategic selling approaches like Rule 1-52-X™ to ensure you always have new lead flow for contact.

4. While you may be maxed at any given time with administrative or time consuming account development activities, you can still stay in contact with your database and keep yourself virtually seen in the selling pipeline flow.

5. You will look more strategic and bigger in your marketplace by being able to deploy much more effectively, thoroughly and consistently strategic selling approaches like Rule 1-2-3-4-5-X ™ to ensure you stay connected in the follow-up measures to the contacts, leads, clients, COIs, etc. in your marketplace.

6. You can use the database to search for hot prospects or high value contacts in a specific geographical area when setting appointments. This ensures your time is highly maximized and that all travel routes are highly populated with high value contacts along the way. Why have a long drive to one appointment when you can plan multiple appointments.

7. If database management is taking place, when a fellow colleague is out sick or leaves, then account maintenance is easier to administrate and possible hot leads can be quickly identified and harvested from others' database systems.

8. Your database should give you significant contact intelligence from buying history, buying ability, referral or COI opportunities, competitor awareness opportunity from this contact, etc.

9. From a sales management perspective, ineffective use of a database can also show where a person may need additional professional development, coaching or counseling.

My experience, whether selling at the Fortune 100 level, within Armed Forces Recruitment, Association Management and

Fundraising, or as a solo professional services practitioner, is that a database is golden.

The database is a life-sustaining component of the sales professional organizational structure for today and tomorrow.

Chapter 51

Performance Driven Selling©
Strategic Selling via Tracking
Your Account Activity and
Status Using The "Sales Contact
Performance Profile" Form

Whether you are working with multiple influencers or decision makers or engaging with one other person, understanding the critical decision points, timelines and breakpoints is critical to establishing your relationship and closing the sale.

The seasoned sales professional understands the significance of information: determining how much one knows concerning any specific account or contact, what competing factors are you selling against (competition, apathy, complacency, urgency, etc.), and recognizing any areas of information deficiency.

Consider a time when a sale was missed or lost due to a lack of knowledge with an account. Maybe with the contact suspect-prospect, incorrect point-of-contact, or missed decision makers in the buying process. Conversely, recognize a time when a sale was made based upon knowing some specific piece of information that the competition lacked – or merely something that someone else failed to recognize or ask.

While some sales professionals maintain an inherent mental "flow chart" of critical information points to attain in the due-diligence phase of a selling activity or prospecting phase, most beginning and junior sales professionals miss this valuable step to sustained selling success.

Consider your mental selling profile of questions you ask or characteristics you know must be present to be engaging a qualified contact. Do you have a written template you work from on each account or contact?

Any thorough profile analysis form should focus questions in several areas:

1. **Actual account contact demographic data profile** (See the database profile form sample in Chapter 50)

2. **Background and historical profile data**

3. **Performance profile relational questions concerning your relationship with the core decision makers** and your position in relationship to making a Close

4. **Time line with the core decision makers** around wanting to make a buying/joining decision

Asking these questions can accelerate your selling and closing ratios.

On the following form sample, the first two sections are self-explanatory Q&A observation points, conversationally gathering or re-confirming this information is rapport building. In the third section, you are scoring your point of contact against the four decision makers to ensure that no decision has been over looked. The second score is to objectively recognize your presentation position with these individual(s) for making a sale, as opposed to any hidden competition points.

By recognizing what you really know and what you may have over looked, you can determine where you are at any given time in respect to:

1. Making a sale
2. What your relationship is with the client or contact
3. What your strength with the client or contact is in relationship to competitors
4. How loyal you are to the client or contact (based upon the volume of knowledge the you have) and how loyal the client may be to you (based upon how little they know about you).

Knowledge is power and the positive application of knowledge in the sales process is a direct connection to your sales profitability.

This knowledge can be gained with first person interaction or with a deeper more global perspective on the account or contact through:

1. **Social Media** sites that the other party uses can give you valuable historical perspective and potential glimpses into where their future aspiration trajectory may be

2. **Historical Data** in your electronic files, data bases, documents, or in-active accounts folders with respect to any prior interactions with that account or contact and your organization, can give you valuable historical perspective and potential glimpses into where their future aspiration trajectory may be

3. **Peers** that you work with or supervisors (business leaders and owners) can give you valuable historical perspective and potential glimpses into where their future aspiration trajectory may be

4. **Competition Analytics** can give you valuable historical perspective and potential glimpses into where their future aspiration trajectory may be

This can aid you in gaining a better more thorough understanding of the other person in respect to their needs, pain-points, urgency for a solution (your solution), and how an association with you will serve them well both now and into their future.

SP3"

sales
CONTACT PERFORMANCE PROFILE

P1 = CONTACT PROFILE

Organization/Firm Name ____
Address ____
City ____
Postal Code ____
Fax ____

Org./Firm Birthday ____
Primary Product/Service/Mission Statement: ____

Secondary Product/Service/Mission Statement: ____

# of Members/Employees ____
Previous Year Earnings/Budget ____

Primary Contact Name ____
Box/Mail Stop ____
State/Province ____
Telephone I ____
Telephone II ____

Contact Birthday: ____

Org./Firm Net Worth ____
Officers' Names ____

P2 = BACKGROUND PURPOSE PROFILE

Product/Solution presented ____
Date of last interaction ____
My position on this is: Exclusive - Dominant - Shared - Below - Unknown
Single objective here is: ____
Secondary objective is ____
Psychological profile ____
Why are they considering my ____
Have I identified all decision makers   YES/NO
Have all levels of the decision loop agreed.   YES/NO/UNKNOWN
Has a decision date been set   YES/NO

Is there a prior relationship here: YES/NO   Competitor(s): ____
Was the outcome a "Win/Win"   YES/NO
Their timing on this is: Urgent - Working on it - No rush - Unknown

Have I visited with each: YES/NO   Can I answer their needs.   YES/NO
Is there interest in my Product/Solution   YES/NO   Is there interest in my competition: YES/NO
Am I using all networking resources: YES/NO   Have I asked for the order: YES/NO

P3 = PERFORMANCE PROFILE

TYPES of BUYERS	CURRENT POSITION	BUYERS ANALYZED	FD✓/✗	BEST STEP	KNOWLEDGE	STAFF x ✓
(T)	(CP)	1				
F-Financial	G-Growth	2				
T-Technical	T-Tender	3				
U-User	S-Stable					
C-Coach/etc.	OC-Over Confident	4				

Jeff Magee International ©

Whether you are engaged in B2B, B2C or P2P relationship building, selling, marketing or COI creation, the data flow from this *Strategic Sales Performance Profile (SP3)* (or a creation of your own) is essential in business and market development and keeping yourself aware of what is happening in your market and with your accounts or contacts.

Chapter 52

Performance Driven Selling©
Exhibit, Trade Show, Display Booth
or Informational Table Venue
Engagement Selling ... Ideas
for Increased Business Opportunities

The opportunity to have suspects, prospects and existing customers funneled directly to you can be a windfall or a crap shoot — you decide.

In reality, most client service representatives, sales professionals, recruiters and business professionals dread working the booth, exhibit, trade show, expo fair, information table more than going to a dentist or paying taxes. However, not taking full advantage of these opportunities is a critical mistake and possibly the greatest career oversight you will ever make.

With a few simple shifts in attitude and behavior, you can turn this informational awareness event into one of the greatest business opportunities you'll ever have.

Having quality and quantity of lead generation at one time and venue can be a strategic accelerator for your business. Instead of dreading these events, view them as B2B, B2C and C2C target rich opportunities. Likewise, this can be an opportunity to re-engage COIs, friends and industry colleagues with increased market exposure. To make this shift in mind and presence for greater ROI consider the following:

264

First, always start with a clear understanding of what your immediate, intermediate and long-term purpose or goal is for exhibiting and showing up.

Second, identify the behaviors of the person who hates the exhibit, fair, display booth, or trade show affairs (and then don't do them). He or she,

1. Shows up late to set up, with an endless list of reasons (aka excuses)
2. Accepts wherever he/she is directed to set up.
3. Creates a display space that is boring or too busy.
4. Spends less time engaging people walking by and more time rearranging the set up. It's amazing how busy one can be at these events . . . doing everything *except* networking and making new valuable qualified leads for later follow-up selling endeavors.

Third, let's turn this event into a cash cow of potential. Here are 25 action plans for your next venue opportunity. If your competition is not taking advantage of this same opportunity, this could be a career-changing experience. In fact, with these *twenty-five plus* strategic and tactical plans, you will find yourself looking for more group venue opportunities.

Get clarity of the B2B and B2C opportunities that differing people that you engage can bring you and engage accordingly. Focus, plan and execute:

1. **It's all about location, location, location.** Get there early and get the high ground. Remember that attendees are not there (just) for you. They are always there to see someone else. Determine who the big players for that venue will be, that your target prospect may be coming to see, and set up next to them. If not relevant, then a great general location would be next to the check-in counter or a high-profile exhibitor. If you are relegated to a low-traffic spot, then the venue should be free. If you yield no meaningful results, make sure the vendor

hosting the event not only refunds your monies, but also gives you bonus exposure in some after-event communication vehicle sent to attendees. In fact, this after-event communication exposure should be sought anyway.

2. **Traffic flow is critical.** Set up so that you are in the early stages of the traffic flow. You don't want to be the first or last booth in a major hall, as the first booth typically intimidates most attendees, and they will purposefully avoid making eye contact with you; by the last booth, most attendees are exhausted and are ready to be somewhere else. Avoid being the left-side placement on corners, as attendees make too fast a turn and will often blast right past you. Ask event promoters or review layout charts to determine what the traffic patterns should be — and then set up in an offensive position. Sometimes there is potential near food stands, but this can sometimes work against you as well. There is an art and a science to traffic flow.

3. **Design a high-energy booth for engagement.** Make sure your display has the energy that attracts — not repels — traffic. Leverage every vantage point as an access point to your booth. Have pictures versus just words; have a television or interactive computer screen playing an endless loop of your most eye-grabbing features and benefit stories. Consider a drawing/giveaway for something, but make sure the prize will be of interest to your ideal prospect/customer. Think like your clients. Have live samples of your product/service if appropriate for tactile interaction; reflect on displays that have drawn you in previously and try to replicate that energy for your display.

One of our clients is the National Guard with an emphasis on the market of 17-to-35-year-old individuals and the Iowa Army National Guard. The Recruiting Commander LTC Higginbotham used what they call their "WOW" tables, using STEM items to generate excitement. Make people fight their way to your display. STEM is science, technology, Engineering and Math. It's a buzz word in education circles.

Tables are set up for interaction and engagement with the market, we have a UAV (unmanned aerial vehicle) called the Raven and its gear on the table, a TOW (tube-launched, optically-tracked, wireless-guided) Missile system, a TV playing a video of cool stuff on a loop, two thermal weapon sites (see through walls, etc.), and a small satellite dish connected to the new high-tech radios.

Once you have a formula for how best to set-up your tables/booths, create a guide and make this the standard. The visual helps your team to learn and execute greatness so as to be able to engage and gather great leads and just meet and build rapport with people you don't know.

4. **Remove all chairs.** Make sure you have no opportunity to withdraw from the audience and let your energy decline. A lot of money is invested in your presence, and the traffic flow is potentially delivering many prospects to meet and follow up on. It would take a month of high-impact prospecting days to equal the potential of this one single event. There will be time to relax when you get home.

    A relaxed stance (sitting) enables you to let your professional guard down, and in many cases, you may engage in dialogue with your booth-mate, thereby ignoring attendees walking by. You are no longer approachable, and many potential prospects will not want to disturb you. Worse even than this are clients walking by, listening to you talk disparagingly about the venue or attendees.

5. **Push your table and display stand screening, etc., to the wall.** Make sure that if you have a booth, any table setup is pushed to the wall. You never want to be hidden behind the table—isolated from the traffic flow—as this makes you less approachable and actually more intimidating.

6. **Offer candy or unique power snack/drink/bar.** Have a sugar fix on your table. Candy attracts as do health bars . . . and chocolate is a magnet.

7. **Set out business cards in three stacks/or a row across the front of the table.** Make sure you have your business contact cards in three different stacks across your display area, not just in one area. This way, if you are blocking one stack or engaged in a dialogue in front of another stack, a passerby will be able to see other cards, increasing the odds that he or she will pick one up and contact you later.

8. **Make a personalized business card brochure.** For every person you meet, take one of your own business cards, and on the reverse side, draw a circle in the middle. In the circle, write the prospect's name and date, and on the outside of the circle, draw axis lines outward. On each line (draw as many as you need), write down the greatest feature and benefit items you can offer for that particular prospect.

9. **Limit your table brochures.** Don't have so much literature on your table that it looks like a warehouse. Only give brochures, flyers, catalogs, etc. that are truly appropriate for each particular suspect or prospect. Make sure you write the person's name in at least two different places, referencing at least two major print items of specialized interest to the suspect's/prospect's needs. By writing the name in the material, you increase

the likelihood of your literature actually going home with and being read by the potential customer.

10. **Schedule ten-minute interval meetings/appointments.** Want to fight and eliminate boredom? Here is the most powerful strategic adjustment in your venue set up: instead of going to see customers the week before the exhibit opportunity, schedule them to come by your booth in ten-minute interval appointments. Now you will never be bored, and you will create a continual sense of energy around your booth that will attract greater traffic to your area. Meet with a new client, a center-of-influence/advocate, a hot prospect, someone from whom you need a final signature, a person you were planning to give something to, etc. Stack the cards in your favor. During the event if people need more of your time or specific needs answered, schedule them back like an appointment when you would otherwise be dead, so as to always keep an array of energy and urgency around your space. This attracts others to your space.

11. **Identify the top 25 people you meet during your exhibit and develop a separate campaign to mail them a series of collateral (hard copy, tangible) pieces for two months.** This could include a simple hand-written "Thank You Note" within 24-hours of your event, then one week out a brochure or flyer that follows up on something you discussed with them, followed up two weeks later by another informational piece on you and or your organization, followed up three weeks later by one final value rich media piece. Along with each of these mailed out pieces, you can enhance the power and influence of this campaign by making a follow-up telephone call to move that contact forward into active customer status.

12. **Consider the nature of the venue** you exhibited at and the real reason individuals have attended the event (it

probably wasn't just to see you). With that goal clearly in mind, now evaluate if you have any complimentary information, services, or products to assist them in their endeavors, and if so make sure you send that to them as value added differentiator and a simple note, "FYI".

13. **Make sure you likewise send a hand-written "Thank You Note" to the sponsor of the event** that you were invited to exhibit at, as well as the actual Venue operator them self, as a way of expressing your appreciation for the opportunities they afforded to you. This will also be a shock to them as no one ever thinks about them afterwards, and will serve as a stock raising action with the sponsor and allow you greater courtesies for the next event.

14. **Check with the sponsor of the event to see if they maintain a master list of attendees** or members over-all to their organization (business, association, community, etc.) and inquire about penning a content rich (no self promotion here) value added article for their newsletter, journal, magazine, or electronic news services (eZine or blog). Inquire about having this appear in the publication to these people immediately after having exhibited (or posted to their website). This becomes a major differentiator and serves as a second party endorsement of you to this demographic.

15. **To make action item twelve more impactful, inquire about offering a column for publication in any media piece prior to the exhibit trade show opportunity that the sponsor may have.** This will serve as a subtle pre-marketing endeavor, and people may seek you out at the exhibit venue because of a compelling editorial item you wrote about.

16. **Immediately after every exhibit opportunity debrief (either by yourself, or with your colleagues) what worked, what did not work, and what you could have**

done to make the experience more productive. Identify from that same venue opportunity what exhibitors seemed to be significantly more attractive to participants, and then determine how you can replicate that in your booth the next time, and even better yet, how can you surpass that at your next event. If there is a member of your team whose personality is better suited for future events, make sure they are present the next time.

17. **If you had a give-away item, now evaluate whether it was a flash-in-the-pan item that people may have grabbed while there, yet thrown away as they left the exhibit area. If so never spend your money on that item again. Determine who had something so original that** people went out of their way to go by their exhibit area to get it, and better yet they will be using it throughout the conference and afterwards. This will improve your exposure into their circle of influence when they go back home and continue to use them. For example, the United States ARMY gives new enlisted recruits in route to basic training black shoulder back-packs with a big gold star and the simple word ARMY on the back - I have seen these on youth's shoulders all over the place and on the shoulders of parents, business people, and soldiers in airports, malls, and on the streets, all of whom are not the target audience yet act as a walking advertisement.

At a recent exhibit in Jacksonville, Florida they handed out florescent-colored padded grips with their website name on them for participants to place around the handles of their pull briefcases and luggage. The Toronto Canada Chamber handed out classy leather-bound travel shoe shining kits. Another exhibit vendor handed out meal tip calculators printed on the reverse of their business card onto a plastic credit card sized handout.

18. **If you feel appropriate, partner with a complimenting exhibitor (maybe even a competitor) to exchange leads after the exhibit opportunity.** Then send to those contacts that you have cross referenced to ensure that they are duplicates a letter that simply reads, **"Your name was given to me after the _____ *(insert the name of the event you exhibited at here)* _____ event you attended, it was suggested to me to contact you _____ *(insert a powerful benefit statement here)* _____. If this sounds like something that you would like to hear more about, please give me a call at _____ or send me an email to _____. Thank you for your time."** By doing this you can morph your contact list and extend your reach from having exhibited.

19. **Contact the sponsor of the event (ideally you would have done this before the event) and see if you can have access to their invitation list** for the event or membership list. If you can get the contact list or access to their list, send them a pre-invitation to stop and see you, and a post follow up invitation to connect with you.

20. **Duffel Bag/Back-Pack Display.** Imagine you are a military enlistment recruiter, bring your duffel bag or ruck bag and spread out across your table or display booth items of your actual life (i.e. night vision goggles, gloves, shovel, paint, food …), instead of the expected hand-out items as *this will induce a higher level of curiosity* and allow you to engage attendees and prospects in a more meaningful manner. So, what is your Duffle-bag equivalent?

21. *Work the other Vendors at the event,* as they may be more valuable prospects or lead generators (Centers-of-Influence/COIs), than they attendees you initially came to meet.

22. *Use Social Media* (*Twitter, Facebook, LinkedIn, etc.*) to promote the event and share where you will be, why, and what early bird attendees will receive when they connect with you. Have your COIs forward your social media messages to their contacts. Then use it continuously while at your event to show high energy interactions and booth engagement to excite others to attend now or follow-up with you at a later date. Ask visitors to post their experience to their social media.

23. *VIP Meet-and-Greet or Q&A Interview, Invite A Celebrity Personality/Your Boss/and Subject-Matter-Expert (SME) to be at Your Spot.* Be smart about your time and leverage the people who can make the space more exciting. If you are a military Recruiter have one of or several of your most recent enlistments/soldiers present to create a buzz, work the room and invite people back to the table/booth, display their contacts and leverage their social media contacts to stop by. Have theses invited co-hosts at your Table to wear their new uniforms or paint their faces in war wear, etc.

24. **Calendar Your Event.** Cross reference the venue hosting group's calendar, against any community calendar against your calendar to ensure that you maximize your exposure, marketing efforts and what assets (people, collateral materials, give away media pieces, etc.) to make this event as productive as possible.

25. **Draw attention to your space,** by being professional and yet memorable in your presence. Helium balloons can attract attention from across the room to your space, especially of you are in the back or a crappy location; Place traditional 4 to 6 foot floor banners on your table and you'll gain 4 more feet of air borne visibility; Have a power recharging station, water, unique and usable trinkets/give-away items; Have a Celebrity personality present; Have show-and-tell items out that people would typically never see or be able to experience as attention and energy creators ...

Selling via exhibits, display booths, BOR, informational setups like a fair, conference, trade show or on-line virtual meeting spot, should be seen as a blitzing opportunity to meet, greet, engage, sell or recruit people for future follow-up.

Change your attitude and create a power force that compels people to stop by, and you'll see more people in a shorter time frame . . . thus increases your yield.

Chapter 53

**Performance Driven Selling©
Brand Management - Percentage
of Market Share in Prospect's
& Customer's Mind That You
Own Impacts Percentage of Sales
You Make in Your Market**

W hat others say about you, tells the world who you are. This is Brand identification.

Ensuring market dominance for your product and services both in the immediate term and future is based upon what percentage of the prospect and customer mind-share you own.

So, what does this mean? *Think Brand-Management.* Take a Nano-second pop quiz, do any of the following confuse you or leave you wondering who they are or what the offer:

1. If you see the *NIKE* swoosh emblem on an article of clothing or printed in an ad, do you know what the swoosh represents?
2. How about the name or icon *AMAZON*?
3. And *IBM*?
4. How about the *INTEL* music jingle on television or radio?

5. And the **Golden Arches** is who?
6. What are **eBay's** colors?
7. Ever heard of **Facebook?**
8. What about **Google?**

Each of these have been branded to such a level that they occupy market share in your head - mindshare. If and when the time comes that you may need a product or service that you know or believe they would provide, there is a greater likelihood that you will go to them, versus someone you have never heard of, even if that provider is more convenient to you.

You never get a second chance to make a first impression.

Gaining market share in someone's head (mindshare) is a process and you should take every opportunity available. We know that our mind creates/send and interprets/receives messages in one of three core ways. Here's how to utilize them:

1. **Visual** –visually communicate (sight) with your audience whenever possible.
   a. Explore every conceivable way that you can touch the market in a visual manner. Then identify which ones are appropriate to utilize.
   b. See how your competition is reaching and influencing people to take action and use this as a benchmark.

2. **Auditory** – utilize auditory communication (sound) with your marketplace whenever possible.
   a. Explore every conceivable way that you can touch the market in an auditory manner. Then identify which ones are appropriate to utilize.
   b. See how your competition is reaching and influencing people to take action and use this as a benchmark.

3. **Kinesthetic** – utilize kinesthetic or the face-to-face or interactive manners whenever possible.

a. Explore every conceivable way that you can touch the market in a a kinesthetic manner. Then identify which ones are appropriate to utilize.

b. See how your competition is reaching and influencing people to take action and use this as a benchmark.

As you explore the many ways to use these three strategies, make sure you:

1. **Are Consistent and Repetitive,** you can't change your logo, name, or mantra on a regular basis and expect to gain, maintain or even grow market share in your prospect's or client's mind.

   Research also reflects the importance of multiple mindshare impressions to motivate others to recall you and take action towards you. Know your magic number of impressions.

2. **Are Appropriate,** consider your market by gender, age, ethnicity, geography, social-economics, profession-trade, education-experience, etc. and make sure your message does not put you in a hostile position with the market and create negative market share in someone's mind.

3. **Position Based Upon all 4-USFs**, make sure that what you do reaches a Unique Selling Factor (aka unique selling proposition) with the recipient. This can be done by positioning what you offer in others' minds by being: Different; Faster; Cheaper (cost effective); Better than what they are either presently receiving in the market place or what they can get in the market place.

4. **Use COIs & Client Testimonials and Networks Effectively**, identify and call upon your Centers-of-

Influence (also known as advocates, allies, champions) regularly to defend you, sell you, promote you. Use their names and likeness in as many visual postings as possible and leverage them and their centers of influence within the market place.

5. **Use Rule 3-3-30®**, marketers believe that you have 3-seconds to capture someone's attention, another 3-seconds for the recipient to determine if your offer is appropriate to them, and if so then they will invest about 30-seconds to read and determine a value proposition to them. That means you have 36 seconds to gain market share or die.

As you launch campaigns to generate greater market awareness, or to change buying habits, or create market change, these KPIs can be powerful guideposts. Have an automated system, customer database system or an Excel spreadsheet of the differing demographic contacts for connectivity campaigns and reach as appropriate.

Out of sight equals out of mind in today's fast-paced branding world and call-to-action selling universe.

To get greater market share of the mind, you must speak to "them" and not about "you" in what you do. Here's an exercise to determine whether your message (via printed materials, radio or television ads, electronic deliverables, etc.) is focused on your audience.

Use two different color markers to highlight every line of your marketing materials. Use one color to shade all words/message that speak about you, and a second color to shade all words/message that speak about them. When completed, the color shades for "them" should be significantly greater than the "you" (which is code for me, me, me text).

Now take these ideas and intensify and magnify your market reach by empowering everyone in your organization or network to become *force multipliers* to your initiatives. Ask them to reach out to their contacts and networks on your behalf.

The old adage of, "Little things mean a lot" is no longer valid in attaining mental market share. Now it is, "Little things mean everything".

Chapter 54

Performance Driven Selling©
Becoming the Expert.
Self-Proclaimed Professional
or Hack?

Engaging a real expert allows you to quantifiably accelerate your rate of failure and your rate of success. As a selling professional, you must position yourself as a real expert.

In today's robust internet world, traditional B2B, B2C, C2C commerce and need for immediate consumption, the depth of the marketplace subject matter experts and apparent influencers are astonishing. It is like a "kiddie pool of true intellect, understanding, experience and credibility." Yet most people seem to either be oblivious or are so complacent that they just check out.

Today, what passes for an expert or person of legitimate credentials, would have ten years ago been called a "new hire, a beginner or a neophyte." With the aging Baby-Boomer population and entrance of the Millennials and Generation-Z rapidly overtaking the majority of the workforce over the next five years, it is estimated that nearly sixty-percent of those in managerial-leadership and "boss" positions in 2001 will be retired and gone by 2020.

Generations of Americans were reared with cultural mantras such as: work hard, apply yourself, always learn, have self-respect, achieve, help others, operate from etiquette, and you will be rewarded. This created the mindset of AmeriCAN. Today, we have a generational and cultural mindset of "reward me first and maybe I'll work hard later."

As a consumer you expect a doctor, nurse, medical professional, attorney, engineer, realtor, pilot, accountant, consultant, etc., to have advanced formal educational degrees in their practice area and participate in on-going professional development endeavors.

This should be expected of selling professionals as well.

With the rise of self-proclaimed experts and wannabes, be careful where you get your "education" from and make sure you are a good steward of others. Consider the company you keep and the company you access. Consider these vetting observations and questions to unearth the real expert from the self-proclaimed. Then apply these questions to yourself and figure out how you measure up as a selling professional.

1. Have you ever done or consumed what you are selling as an apprentice or beginner? Can you prove it?
2. Have you ever done it as a journeyman or employee/member?
3. Have you ever done it as a master or leader?
4. Can you prove anything based upon fact, data and logic versus emotion, rhetoric and assertions?
5. What would ten of your reputable clients/benefactors say about your deliverables?
6. Is there a degree in your area of specialty and do you have it?
7. Is there a trade association certification in your area of specialty and do you have it?
8. Have they ever been featured in a credible third-party publication or newswire about your specialty?
9. Have you ever penned a White Paper on your specialty?

10. If appropriate, have you ever authored a book which was published by a credible and reputable publisher?
11. Have you ever designed, written, implemented and taught an instruction course in which you are a self-proclaimed expert?
12. Do you hold a patent, trademark or a copyright certificate on your body-of-work, expertise or deliverable?
13. Are you the innovator of anything in your subject matter, or are you an imitator of others work?
14. Have you ever spoken before a body of peer experts in this space?
15. If I go to your website, will it prove you are professional?
16. Have you actually had tremendous wins and failures in your profession?
17. And above all, Can YOU Prove It?

This is how to catch a self-proclaimed expert wannabe in the act of embellishment or straight-out B.S.:

1. What would someone learn if they fact check your resume or LinkedIn Profile. If you do not have one, that may be a major clue.
2. Have you harvested others' credentials and body-of-work as your own?
3. Check the social media world for profiles and begin the process of reverse reading. You can add more content to the social media world to bury past trails, but it is very difficult to make data disappear. If your employment changes with the seasons, you need evidence for why you are not a charlatan.
4. Check the credentials, pedigree, experiences cited and make sure the math adds up.
5. If someone were to ask for several references. If you hesitate or can't provide multiple client references, this is a major red flag – others should run from you.

6. A major clue you are a self-proclaimed expert that can't sustain an ROI will be your resistance and persistent deflection to other topics.
7. What if you are in an interview and are asked for copies of the past employer-employee performance reviews for discussion or a copy of your most recent tax statement – these are major reality checks.

Accountability matters, and how you create or abdicate accountability is critical. You may receive pushback when others see you as the self-proclaimed expert. If you see any of these red flags in your history, you may be acting disingenuous:

1. Culture (generational, ethnicity, regional, diversity, etc.) will be re-written to justify your outcome with no sense of personal ownership and personal responsibility.
2. Values will be abdicated.
3. Deflection (deflect responsibility and blame someone else) away from them self and the core matter by playing the blame game to make someone else the problem and positioning them self as the victim.

Performance success creates clear mandates and dictates. The ramifications of actions, accountability or lack of accountability on you and others when influenced by a self-proclaimed expert is devastating. Successful individuals will not stay within an organization that maintains and sustains this environment. If you are the self-proclaimed expert, it's time to do something meaningful, contribute something meaningful, and get a job. If you have never done anything, don't proclaim to have done so – step aside and let the real innovators/adults lead the way.

Engaging a real expert allows you to quantifiably accelerate your rate of success. A real expert serves as a force multiplier to you. Engage a sage as coaches for daily or weekly check-ins and accountability growth opportunities. Identify mentors to develop and guide your growth. Create peer groups that are comprised of people with greater credentials than you to serve as a 360° benchmark for excellence in all that you do. Develop a balanced

IQ and EQ with substantial readings and continuous mental DNA enrichments on a regular basis. And, explore all opportunities to mentally tithe to others – but only those that will appreciate you and pay-it-forward.

Just as complacency and mediocrity grows contempt, so too can success beget success.

Chapter 55

**Performance Driven Selling©
View Your Customers Via a
Frequent Customer Program Matrix**

It's not really a new idea, from main steer USA general stores of the frontier days to the cyber world of today, businesses must be mindful of their customers, trends, demographics, likes, needs and desires. The analytics of your customers reveal where your business is now and where it will be tomorrow. Recognizing that all customers are not equal and learning how to build a lasting, sustainable business with followers (fans, advocates, centers-of-influence, tribes, etc.) is critical to market share and market dominance.

The analytics and concept is easy. You stratify customers (constituents, membership, consumers) based upon value, importance, ROI, etc., and can then generate deeper analytics on every aspect of your business from the feedback, engagement and interactions.

Frequent Customer Loyalty Programs allow for a better business client relationship, that is predicated upon multiple objectives – reward current clients with premiums to say 'thank you' and give them reasons to partner with you, and to generate new business by pulling consumers away from your competition. These programs can be built to show cross synergies and provide real time analytics for your business.

Today we can see variances of the loyalty marketing campaign across every aspect of the B2B and B2C market place.

The smart sales professional realizes that there will always be a second transaction from every customer in their life time and that every customer can also become an advocate if so motivated. Viewing every customer through the lens of the frequency customer transaction model can give you valuable ways to increase your market awareness, presence, and effectiveness. Your competition is aware of this. You should be as well.

As an example, in the past ten years, I have purchased three homes. Every transaction was done by a different sales professional and different real estate Broker. Why? Simple, none of the Realtors showed appreciation for my business and none had a system in place to stayed connected. Not one agent or broker even sent a Thank You note after the transaction. Why would I reward their obvious bush league behavior with another transaction?

Whether you get an appointment, a sales presentation opportunity, a sale, or a "no", what does your follow-up behavior reveal about you? More sales are made after the "no" and after the two of you have long since parted company, than have been made on the first interaction.

Call the tiers of acknowledgement whatever you like, the formulas are always the same. You can build your Frequent Customer Program like a matrix with:

1. *Platinum's - Most Valuable Customers/Contacts:* Differing rewards, awards (tangible and intangible), acknowledgements, communications, opportunities, access, privileges, courtesies, invitations, upgrades, thank you, differing price-breaks, allowances, give-backs, premiums, etc.

2. *Gold's – Next Most Valuable Customers/Contacts:* A downgrade of options from your top tier acknowledgements, yet enticing enough to have a greater mindshare for you and less for others in the marketplace ...

3. *Silver's – Next, Next Most Valuable Customers/Contacts:* A downgrade of options from your next to the top tier acknowledgements. You are rewarding these constituents for aligning with you in their early stage of marketplace transactions, and the greater the incentive to work with you, the greater your market growth can become in steering them away from the competition.

Each of these premiums would be based upon differing levels of patronage and designed to induce greater patronage. Whether your organization actually has a formal initiative like this or not, the sooner you start recognizing that the marketplace is comprised of individuals that can affect your business at these volume levels, the sooner you will strategically see and engage the marketplace.

You can start to benchmark your efforts off the top tier (Platinum's) in everything that you do to attract more of the customers best suited for what you have to offer. When you have exhausted all you can do for that demographic, you can concentrate on the next tier (Gold's) to develop a thriving business sales pipeline/funnel.

Build your model today and launch it immediately. Your customers are on the line.

Chapter 56

**Performance Driven Selling®
Building Lasting Sales Relationships
by Providing "Reliable C.A.R.E.™"
To Every Customer: Five Ways
to Build Immediate and Lasting
Credibility with a Client**

Building customer loyalty is essential to effective long-term selling. Studies repeatedly illustrate that it takes more time, money and energy to gain one new customer, than to keep an existing customer.

For several years and across three continents, while conducting Service-Leadership© focused executive development programs, *JEFF MAGEE INTERNATIONAL/JMI, Inc.* (now www.JeffreyMagee.com) surveyed and collected information from more than 10,000 participants on customer service issues. Surveyed questions:

1. "When you are the customer and spend your hard-earned money, what do you look for from the vendor you go to?

2. "Conversely, if they did not provide you "X," would you look for another vendor-partner?"

The research project across the United States, Canada, Australia, Europe and England revealed that customers measure their loyalty to a vendor/individual based upon the vendor's credibility. And credibility is measured in a combination of five ways.

This model is called the *"Reliable C.A.R.E™"* formula. You need to measure yourself personally against this model and then measure the others in your organization who deal with your customers (other sales professionals, customer service coordinators, billing representatives, receptionists...). However, until you pass all five categories, don't talk to your colleagues about their shortcomings.

Whether you are engaged in B2B, B2C, C2C exchanges or deliver from a virtual or traditional market variables, customers want to do business with credible people and organizations (aka Vendor's, You). Credibility is measured from the customer's perception of your ability to meet or exceed these five measurement categories:

1. *Reliable* - how reliable are you and what you represent? Do you deliver what you say you will? Do you do what you say you will? Do you produce what you say you can? Do you deliver on what's expected of you by the consumer? This is one of many factors that create your brand – what does your brand tell the market about you and what you represent?

2. *Care/Caring* - does the customer feel that you genuinely care for them, appreciate them, respect them, understand them, have their best interest in mind? Of all of the responses in our survey, the number one responses were 'appreciate' and that falls into this second category – CARE.

3. *Attractive* - are you and your organization an attractive option to them as compared to others in the market place? Do you meet or exceed the initial expectations of

the customer? Do you look professional, act professional, sound professional, standout as best-in-class, etc.?

4. *Responsive* - does the prospect or client feel that you address their needs in a timely manner? Do you deliver and follow-up in a time frame which is expected or ahead of expectations? Are you accessible to them and the marketplace? What touch points do you have and can you become more accessible and transparent in your connectivity to the marketplace?

5. *Empathy* - does the customer feel as if you understand and acknowledge their position or views? Are you genuine or phony? Do you make them feel safe in your presence?

If you look at any new WOW business that grabs market attention and accelerates its' traction to success, you will find that they are merely providing the marketplace **Reliable C.A.R.E.** And conversely, if you study any institution that has failed and disappeared from the marketplace, they failed because they failed the **Reliable C.A.R.E.** variables. The consumer is easy to please... and not very forgiving when you fail.

Another way to benchmark yourself off of best-in-class actions, trade industry reference points, and what your best profile clients/customers expect, is to look into each category of the **Reliable C.A.R.E.** for endless ideas and answers.

Imagine:

1. YOU are an *Association* and you are looking to evaluate why people love you (want to join, advocate you to their circle of influence and followers and give freely as they can) or hate you (aka are not attracted to you or to come back a second time to you), run the model and solicit feedback?

2. YOU are a *Start-Up Business* and you are looking to evaluate why people love you (want to patronize your establishments, advocate you to their circle of influence and followers and re-engage you freely as they can) or hate you (aka are not attracted to you or to come back a second time to you). Run the model and solicit feedback.

3. YOU are a *Military Leader* and you are looking to evaluate why people love you (want to be a part of your Unit/Company/Command) and are proactively happily engaged or hate you (appear complacent, disengaged, bitter and never appear proactive in your Unit/Company/Command and look for the least to do for the maximum paycheck and are any winner is fast tracking themselves out of your presence). Run the model and solicit feedback.

4. YOU are an *Established Business* and you are looking to evaluate why people love you (want to patronize your establishments, advocate you to their circle of influence and followers, re-engage you freely as they can, and speak constructively about you to their on-line platforms) or hate you (aka are not attracted to you or to come back a second time to you, and speak ill about you to their on-line platforms). Run the model and solicit feedback.

If you can use this **Reliable C.A.R.E.** formula as a benchmark in evaluating your personal engagements with customers and score high marks in each category, then and only then do you arrive at the right to hold your peers accountable to deliver the same.

Consider designing a fast, simple evaluation grid for each of these "letters" and asking your valued customers to occasionally score you. Compare their feedback to how you would have scored yourself. You can use a score template of:

1. 0-points = did not meet customer expectations

2. 1-point = met customer expectations
3. 2-points = exceeded customer expectations

You could further enhance the effectiveness of such a score grid by asking the same **Reliable C.A.R.E.** formula questions for both the human equation (you) and the product equation (what they received that you delivered or facilitated).

Your customer's responses become your litmus test as to whether you are meeting or exceeding their expectations and delivering the services or products to the best of your abilities.

This is a powerful means to influence the DNA of an organization to become W.O.W.® (the original 2003 book of the same name, https://www.amazon.com/Beyond-WOW-Defining-Customer-Service/dp/0971801037/ref=sr_1_1?s=digital-text&ie=UTF8&qid=1506784637&sr=8-1&keywords=wow+book+by+jeffrey+magee) oriented and Service-Leadership focused.

This formula can be used as a template when interacting with any customer. You can reference any or all of these categories when designing a survey questionnaire. Customer feedback, whether positive or negative, can be valuable in determining future courses of action and interaction.

This insight can also aid in determining future product or service expansions, and where to make additions and improvements to satisfy the customer and improve your core business.

In today's fast paced, highly competitive market place, your only advantage may be your credibility ... do you truly provide customers with *"Reliable C.A.R.E™"*?

Chapter 57

Performance Driven Selling©
The 4-Core Reasons Customers
Leave and Prospects Don't Buy

U nderstanding the psychology of the marketplace towards you and your Deliverable/Offer is critical in determining how to promote, engage and connect with the market to make a sale or repeat sale. This understanding also impacts your ability to win back lost clients and advocates.

You can do a deep dive for your industry as to the core psychological "logic" reasons for decisions and you can perform the same on the "emotional" level of reasons for decisions that align to you or away from you. Research reflects that there are four dominant "emotional" reasons that tend to tip a decision in one direction or another. Then, the customer or prospect looks for evidence or "logic" to re-affirm their decisions.

In addition, customers leave for one of four core reasons (typically "emotional" reasons at the outset). These may be the same reasons that prospects are not attracted to you. The psychology of winning and losing the sale sits within the mind of the person that you are engaging. These four reasons can cause us to lose a customer if someone makes them a better offer.

Consider your presentation flow, reflect on what and how you say what you say, and align that with the four driving reasons that a customer or prospect may be engaging you. People typically are looking to maintain or gain:

1. **Better** – Natural tendency is for individuals to want equal to or better in their next transaction from their last transaction. How do you convey that what you have is better than other market options?

2. **Faster** - individuals want equal efficiencies to or more efficient/faster in their next transaction from their last transaction. How do you convey that what you have is more efficient/faster than other market options?

3. **Different** - individuals want an edge over others and to not look exactly like others. They want a differentiator in their next transaction from their last transaction. How do you convey that what you have is markedly different and thus worth the change?

4. **Cost-Effective/Financial** - individuals want the "biggest bang for their buck" or more for less in their next transaction from their last transaction. How do you convey that what you have is more financially beneficial than other market options?

If you look and feel just like everyone else in the marketplace, then why should someone change from where they are doing business and transition to you? Or, if someone is a prospect, why should they entertain your offer over what they are presently receiving and where they are comfortable. Or worse yet, why should a complacent prospect not doing business with anyone all of a sudden be motivated to become a customer if they don't believe you can make their quality of professional or personal life – Better, More Efficient, Different or more Financially rewarding?

Reflect on your pre-marketing materials sent into a marketplace, your marketing messaging sent to an identified contact, your social media messaging, what is conveyed from your website statements/images/video/posts/etc., what you actually ask the prospect to reveal how (from their perspective) each of these are being addressed. Identify how you address and defend these in your presentation or proposal, and all of your follow-up messaging and call-to-actions.

The more clarity you can gain regarding a customer's or prospect's buying motives (pain or pleasure points) and fundamental needs, the better you can align that with how you communicate your solutions using the four core drivers.

Chapter 58

Performance Driven Selling©
Identifying Why Customers
Love You or Leave You, Via
Your "Customer Service Rating (CSI)"
...It Drives Your Selling Focus and
All Efforts.

M any selling organizations feel that they have customers in because of the great service they offer and or their exclusive product/service. Many times, this may be true, but a sales professionals' understanding of how their organization measures up on an objective **Customer Service Index™ (CSI)**, may reveal why a customer truly does business with them and why that same customer may leave.

Building customer loyalty today is an extremely difficult task. Just providing a customer with "Excellent" customer care alone may actually cause a customer to leave. To ensure that a customer gained is a customer maintained, sales professionals and internal customer care agents must continuously strive to provide "Exceptional" customer care.

Consider the following CSI. Customers measure your deliverables on two basic variables. On a scale of low to high, based upon where these two variables measure, dictates how the prospects/customers buying or repeat buying decision take place and directly influence a buyers' loyalty.

CUSTOMER SERVICE INDEX (CSI)

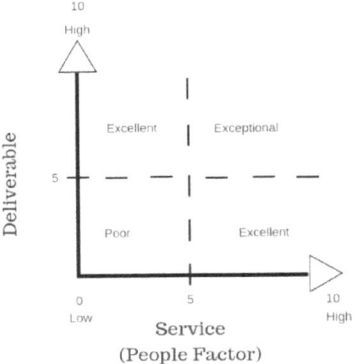

Here is how the CSI impacts your ability to make a sale, increase selling frequency, impacts COI development, generate referrals or create analytics that will aid you in forecast analysis for market trends.

Start by using the CSI diagram to measure how a customer might rate the actual product or service being purchased on the vertical axis, from low at the bottom to progressively better the higher up the scale the feedback reveals (maybe a scale of 0-4.9 low scores and 5-10 high scores). Then, measure the way the people associated with that transaction handled that encounter (maybe a scale of 0-4.9 low scores and 5-10 high scores).

To label the four differing quadrants and understand how some of the traditional labels for customer care may actually be very deceiving and thus lead to maybe a sale or win now, and massive lost business tomorrow, consider:

1. A CSI score in the bottom left quadrant would be labeled **"POOR"** customer care and would obviously lead to lost business. This indicates that the brand promise made was not met in the actual deliverable and

the human interaction aspects failed to meet customer expectations as well.

2. A score in the bottom right quadrant would be labeled **"Excellent"** customer care. Although the product or service they are buying, receiving or affiliating with didn't meet or exceed their expectations, sometimes it is the sales professional that maintains the business and in essence carries the organization. This really indicates more of an affinity to the CSR/people in the interaction and thus the relationship is more based upon the serving person/CSR/Agent than the company or business deliverables. This is a dangerous relationship transaction to find yourself in, as the client is loyal to the person and not the deliverable or organization. If the representative leaves your selling organization, the customer may as well. Keep in mind that when the customer says anything positive, like you do an "excellent" job, this may actually be misleading.

3. A score in the top left quadrant would be labeled **"Excellent"** customer care also. Again, a very misleading label, and the sales professional must understand that business is taking place because of product loyalty/brand loyalty and not because the sales professional is delivering great care. This too can lead to future lost business. Here the brand or deliverable is carrying the transaction

4. The ultimate goal of every sells professional is to have a CSI score in the top right quadrant. This is when the product/service/deliverable and the sales professional/people touch-points both exceeded the customer's expectations (a minimum score on both CSO axis lines of 5.1) and is labeled, **"Exceptional"** customer care.

From an organizational standpoint, you must recognize that customers doing business with you that score in the bottom right quadrant, leave your bottom line statistics when their sales professional leaves. The same is true for top left quadrant business. As soon as another vendor enters your market with an equal product/service, the customers will leave in droves. They may be frustrated with giving their money and business to an organization where they feel unappreciated.

As a sales professional, you must strive for business transactions to be top right quadrant activities. These are advocates of you and your organization, a culture of inclusiveness and excited customers, and an energy that feeds your selling pipeline/funnel for a healthy today and tomorrow. Again, top right quadrant indicators reveal this is where the customer feels appreciated, valued, and involved, like their personal needs are being met and that the deliverables are doing as advertised.

Challenge yourself to achieve higher vertical and horizontal axis scores. Exceed your customer's expectations and needs. Judge yourself against the four core reasons that customers leave or aren't attracted in the first place. Is the product/service:

1. Better than what others are receiving or what they received last time
2. A faster or more efficient
3. Different
4. Cost-Effective

A sales professionals' understanding of how their organization measures up on an objective **Customer Service Index™ (CSI),** according the consumer, may reveal why a customer truly does business with them and why that same customer may leave.

Always strive to have and leave every client interaction in the top right quadrant.

Chapter 59

Performance Driven Selling©
Applying the BLENDS™
Model in Re-Building Credibility
When Your Product, Service
or Organization Has Bottomed
Out in The Market's Mind

As a sales professional you realize that your market has a bad taste in their mouth for your offer and organization. There is a way to overcome this.

Your first objective is not to win them back as customers or champions (Centers-of-Influence) but rather to re-condition the market to take another look and re-evaluate their perceptions of you. It's back to basics. You'll have to sell yourself and earn the markets trust of you 'personally' before they will reconsider your organization and offers.

Consider the following actions plans:

1. Archive a specific list of market concerns, reactions, opinions of you and your organization that has left a negative imprint on them. Don't take this market research or exit-interviews of lost recent clients personally, it is their perspective and at this point, remember the adage – Perception is Reality.

2. Then before you contact the market, ensure that you have addressed the most significant issues and concerns with yourself and all of the stake-holders within your organization. Determine sequential steps to address, respond, engage in damage control, and demonstrate with resounding examples and evidence that you are not as the perceptions reveal and that you are worthy.

3. To make sure you have righted this 'credibility gap', become a mystery customer to your own organization and learn first-hand if the concerns have been rectified. If you experience any challenges, imagine how this will be amplified in the eyes and mind of the market that already has a negative view of you. You may get a second opportunity to win them back, but you will not get a third.

Do you want to win back the market one strategic high impact influencer at a time or make a major community splash? Consider the following six tactical wins back options:

1. **B – Boost** - A Boost from a satisfied customer can serve as a reason to make an instant telephone call, send an email, text or leverage a post within social media. Your reference to the satisfied customer or a recommendation from them, may serve as the most valuable re-contact.

2. **L – Letter -** Craft a thoughtful letter or series of letters as a strategic and quantity regulated direct mail or email contact campaign whereby you introduce yourself as a new person on the scene, acknowledge from your research how your organization (product, service or previous colleagues, without calling anyone out by name) had failed the market in the past. Self-effacing statements of ownership are powerful and then you can transition their heart and mind to the new you and personally invite them to check you out. Leave your contact information, like personal cell number, should

they want to contact you, and let them know that you will be personally contacting them in the next few days to discuss the information and a value-added invitation or offer contained in your letter.

Another iteration of the letter approach could be the re-use of any appreciation letter or email from an enthusiastic client just served, take that content and package it into a letter that you can forward electronically to prospects, with a bounce back (call to action statement or offer), and then follow up with telephone calls or text as appropriate.

3. *E – Examine Evidence* - Re-examine all the evidence; facts, CRM data bases, client files, invoicing, correspondence with predecessors, etc., as to why past clients have left (this is the same for previous Centers-of-Influence lead generators) your organization. If you cannot improve upon the previous problem, don't contact them about returning to your organization. If the evidence reveals that the reasons that they have left have been addressed or the solutions not previously offered are available, then you have earned an opportunity to make contact with them.

4. *N – Needs Analysis* - Offer to administrate a non-fee needs analysis as a value-added service to them. Consider what you have or what abilities individuals within your organization possess and how those could be made available to individual and key prospects one at a time from a value-added perspective? Then, make contact with the market and make that ability available to them as a community service differentiator. Show them how you can assist them and when possible work in a solution offer from your organization.

5. *D – Do something* - The longer you wait to win them back, the faster you will arrive at unemployment or bankruptcy. Take action and do something.

6. *S – Sampling* - Another great way to re-engage lost market contacts, clients, supporters, is to consider what deliverables, services, swag, etc., you have that they may desire. Then offer it to them for free. It's like a free taste test in the grocery store, hard to say no to and chances are that you'll want more of it.

Other ideas for how to approach lost clients, market prospects, and those loyal advocates when the market has soured on you, could be:

1. Have an Open House
2. Have a Theme Party
3. Establish Quarterly events to attract different affinity groups to you
4. Partner with a high impact group, charity, club, etc. that would draw other influencers and possible users of your offer
5. Look for unique places to place your name whereby you can reach new buyers
6. Identify completely new and different markets for your offer that have never heard of you and would not have heard negative things from you from previous disappointed customers
7. Recognize that consumers make their buying decisions based off of any one of four behavioral criteria. Therefore, you have to be able to position yourself so as to convey to the market how your offer is:
   a. Better for them than anything presently available
   b. Faster and therefore more efficient for their needs than anything else presently being made available
   c. Different than anything else presently being offered
   d. Cost effective (cheaper) than what is presently being offered in your brand and quality category

8. Have high influence consumers or community, industry, trade personalities craft an endorsement letter to your target audience on your behalf
9. Make a list of the top ten prospects that you would like to attract and then personally call on them. Reintroduce your organization, product, or services and explain how you have re-committed resources to making this an association they can have confidence in again
10. Look for consumers of your competition right now that may be making an annual or seasonal buying decision. Contact them to introduce yourself as an option for consideration. Ask if you can to contact them prior to their buying decisions time window and then make a note in your information management system to remind you when that time arrives
11. Develop a value-added resource vehicle that you can use to simply stay connected with clients, advocates, prospects, and lost past customers. Maybe it could be a newsletter, value-added blog, an electronic newsletter, a regular direct mail campaign, etc. that provides high impact value to them, and indirectly promotes you. This allows you to stay top-of-their-mind and you may have an opportunity to win their business back in the future. This is a passive action and it may take some time to produce results, however in the big picture and long-term perspective, this can yield significant gains.
12. Schedule follow-up re-occurring touch-point endeavors into Outlook or a system to hold you virtually accountable to do this and continue to do this as necessary.

Joining an organization that is viewed unfavorably by the market is not the end of the world. Don't retreat or feel as if there is nothing you can do. Now is the time to let your professional selling power shine.

Section IV

Leveraging & Beyond the Fundamentals

Chapter 60

Performance Driven Selling©
Why Most Sales Professionals SUC:
Selling is a Profession and
not a Part Time Vocation

Did the title alarm you? Cause your emotional blood pressure to rise? Or better yet, did the title intrigue you?

The difference between SUCCESS and SUC-cess is all about the KPIs one uses, believes in, and holds oneself accountable to daily.

If sales and selling were easy, it would be called Order Taking and the personnel would make a whole lot less. It is called Selling for a reason.

Successful sales professionals in any industry are committed, always engaged in on-going learning, development, and certifications, and are personally benchmarking off of those deemed to be best-in-class.

Consider these macro trends from the world of sales, as published and researched national statistics reveal, and benchmarked against my client observations for three-plus-decades. How do you measure up?

1. 80% of sales are closed/made on/after the fifth contact

2. 48% of sales people never follow up, or don't follow up in a timely manner to have any positive impact on the initial contact activity
3. 12% of sales people make two to three contacts and stop
4. 25% of sales people make a second contact and stop
5. Less than 10% of sales people make more than three contacts with a prospect or lead
6. 2% of sales are made on the first contact
7. 3% of sales are made on the second contact
8. 5% of sales are made on the third contact
9. 90% of sales are made after the fifth engagement, interaction and substantive contact
10. 70% of sales people don't use a system to manage their book of business
11. 80% of sales people have no fundamental selling process when they engage the prospect or client
12. 75% of sales professionals only know 25% of the products/services they represent from a Product IQ perspective
13. Most sales people spend less than 12% of their time on the phone generating leads or making outbound new contacts
14. Monday and Fridays are the slowest days for new business generation for sales professionals, yet most selling professionals have no system to maximize these days for meaningful ROI
15. 98% of all sales professionals that do not make their quotas spend 80% of their time engaged in non-business related social network activities, surfing the internet, and texting personal issues between 8AM and 5PM daily
16. #1 visited/traffic websites Monday through Friday between 8AM and 5PM are pornographic in nature
17. 92% of selling professionals who are not reaching their sales goals spend no time engaging in personal development to better their craft
18. Do you know the math, every selling professional, sales manager and business owner knows their selling math …

a. a. How many general market contacts does it take to get a contract (lead flow analytics)?
b. How many market contacts per SKU does it take to gain/win a contract?
c. How many rapport building calls or non-business meetings does it take to build trust between the prospect and you before serious consideration of your organization or offer takes place?
d. What are the expected and appropriate "no's" a prospect should raise and where in the selling presentation should they arise, and how do you logically address them?
e. How much time, money and resources are invested in gaining one new contract?
f. How much does it cost (or is it an investment) to have you on payroll for twelve months

19. 100% of selling professionals that exceed their selling goals/mission have systems, processes, advisors to ensure their continued accountability and success, and engage in regular reading/listening/studying to improve their craft

What does your picture reveal?

Over the decades I have had the opportunity to work with the top Fortune 500 Firms, mid-cap businesses and start-up entrepreneurial enterprises, along with some of the legends in sales and sales management (*Zig Ziglar, Bill Brooks, Brian Tracy, Jeff Gitomer, Denis Waitley, Harvey Mackay, Mark Victor Hansen and others*), and in every case what I have learned is the above analytics are always correct. Often, the difference between SUCCESS and SUC starts with the mental health we bring to the art and craft of selling and how we apply to ourselves and our environment.

The list of non-business behaviors, nepotism, and biases that derail our potential is alarming. The list above can either ensure our greatness or implode our abilities. In order to improve your sales effectiveness, you must operate like a Sales Professional.

Chapter 61

Performance Driven Selling©
Competitive Analysis of You Versus?
What Do You Know About
Your Competition and What
Do You Know About Your
Deliverable Versus Theirs?

Everyone has competition in some form. A sales professional knows who those competitive challengers are and has well-defined selling plans for competing against them.

You should embrace the challenge and not fear it. Always be ready and confident in addressing competitive challenges and threats as they present themselves.

One powerful way to objectively compare and contrast any specific product, service or your organization over-all in comparison to any primary competitor is to use a *"Ben Franklin Analysis Model."* Legend has it that whenever Benjamin Franklin was challenged and needed to make a decision, he would take a piece of paper, divide it into two equal sides and then label each side of the paper according to the outcomes to the decision. He would then proceed to chronicle all of the positives for each under the appropriate header, then when he was done, he'd choose whichever side had more entries.

You could use the *"Ben Franklin Analysis Model"* to compare strengths/weaknesses organizationally between your organization and number one competitor over-all:

My Org.: _____
Competitor: _____

Strengths/Weaknesses
Strengths/Weaknesses

This same model can be used to compare and contrast products, services or organizational threats to a sales professional line-up in a live presentation before a prospect or client, as well as a mental pre-exercise before engaging the market.

Category: _____
Competitor Category: _____

Strengths/Weaknesses
Strengths/Weaknesses

Successful sales professionals have the ability to objectively look at what they represent and what the competition has to offer. In fact, the more product knowledge that a sales

318

professional has on the competition, the more effective they can become at focusing their prospecting efforts, Selling Presentation skills and in qualifying Suspects as profile potential customers.

When you think in terms of competitive analysis and reflect upon your strengths and weaknesses as compared to a competitor, you can make informed decisions. Here's an example ... Think of a professional sporting teams' coach (your equal as a sales trainer/sales manager/small business owner) on game day. It would be fair to expect that coach to know the name of the opposing team's coach and their primary players, and to have studied the strengths and weaknesses of each and coached their own players on what to expect. The competitive analysis impacts their decisions and choices for how to position themselves for success.

As a sales professional, be your own coach and evaluate your competitive analytics. What do you know and what could blindside you from success?

Your working knowledge is a never-ending learning curve, you can have data on-line, housed in the cloud, or manually at your finger-tips, but what you don't know can be the difference between success, market dominance or finding yourself playing catch-up to others.

Chapter 62

Performance Driven Selling©
Using Surveys to Sell More,
Sell Better & Attract
New Business Opportunities

Imagine that you could discover the major reasons people do business with you and your organization, while simultaneously identifying new selling opportunities?

The strategic use of a survey can produce valuable insights regarding business opportunities, market trends, and early indications as to where you may lose business. The art and science of survey is all about knowing how, where and when to incorporate one of three core survey questions. As a professional sales person, you can deploy survey questions informally to build richer relationships with your clients and the marketplace. Or, you can make these surveys complex technical instruments directed towards specific demographics to solicit explicit information as well.

Let's go low tech and high yield.

There are three different survey questions you can ask. If you'd like to design a detailed survey, you can take these three and drill down with sub-questions or categories.

1. **LIKE** – Always ask the "like" questions first when securing feedback on why someone is doing business with you. If you are talking to a prospect, the "like" question can be used to determine what they are currently getting from their market relationships. Then you'll know what you must meet or beat. The "like" question can also be used when presenting options to someone to identify their dominant buying interest.

   Examples: *What do you like most about how we take care of you? What do you like most about doing business with me/us?; What do you like most about this deliverable?; What do you like most about joining our organization?; What feature do like most about our on-line portal you are using?; With the other vendors/competitors that you do business with, what do you like most about them and how they take care of you?*

   LIKE = **Current $** and why they are doing business with you.

2. **ADD** – Ask this style of questions second if you have time or the other person/group is willing to provide you with additional insights. These are business development questions that reveal where there may be opportunities to do business and provide the customer with more than they present get from their current relationships. Adding these into a conversation, email or structured survey with existing clients, will reveal other business opportunities that you may have missed.

   Examples: *Is there anything else I can do for you today?: Is there anything else you need for your next business project or activity that I can provide to you?; Is there anyone else you know that could benefit from what you have allowed me to serve you with, that you could introduce me to?; It only makes sense if you are doing this, to also consider....?; When would you like to* *place your next order and can I serve you then?; You are making a great decision to join our organization, who else respects and follow you, that you and I should talk to next?; With the other vendors/competitors that call on you, what are they not doing for you, that would be of great value?*

ADD = **More $$** and additional selling opportunities that you may be missing.

3. **STOP/ELIMINATE** – Strategically use these when you have conditioned the market or survey recipient to be non-judgmental, non-emotionally involved and logic focused. These questions are designed to gather deep honest feedback from the other party that typically is not offered freely and early on in relationships. These questions also allow you to uncover possible frustrations and disappointments with clients/members in your business portfolio. Until this information is revealed to you, you can't address it and win the client back. In addition, if you don't find out, it could become a potential future client retention issue. These questions should be asked third as they can be inherently critical or negative.

Examples: *Is there anything that you are having frustrations with at this time with our deliverable or organization?; If you could improve upon one piece of the transaction work with us, what would that be?; If you could eliminate one step in the purchase process, what would that be?; Is there anything that would give you cause to not come back to us for your future business needs?; With the other vendors/competitors that call on you, what do they do that frustrates you the most?*

STOP/ELIMINATE = ZERO $ in the future and where you are about lose clients or run them off from doing business with you.

Integrating these three styles of questions into your conversations, selling presentations, contract/application/order transaction process, phone calls or follow-up emails or letters can ingratiate you to others and provide you with valuable intel to better understand and serve the marketplace.

Think about using these survey questions with your VIP, COIs and top clients on a regular basis. Think about if you or your organization is about to change the way the market does business with you or how you engage the marketplace, these three questions strategically delivered to the right person can give you powerful information to better engage the market or do predictive analysis as to how others will respond, react or be complacent in your next interaction with them.

If you decide to survey your entire client base, data base or a market segmentation, here are a few additional strategic moves to use the feedback appropriately:

1. Code or break down all surveys into two demographics as a macro, the **Vital Few** as your core and most valuable contacts, and the **Useful Many** which are all other contacts or respondents.

2. When you review the responses, consider the source. Do not make a major business change off of the Useful Many, that are not your loyal, best, most valuable clients. While you may get sound feedback from them which may give cause for ancillary business opportunities, new product/deliverable/service extensions, or introductions, if you attack your business based off their feedback, you run the risk of alienating the Vital Few whom are your best.

Do you recall one of the greatest product change debacles in the past Century? COKE eliminated a 100-year old brand for a new flavor. They based this decision off substantial statistical data that people loved the new flavor in taste tests. But they forgot the obvious ... *Who* said they loved it and *who* said they disliked it?

Remember, Useful Many demographics respond the greatest, share the most, and talk the loudest. In most cases, this is also the demographic that is the least loyal and has the greatest degree of apathy, discourse and bitterness as individuals – they are apathetic trend followers.

The way in which you gather survey data will affect the quality of information you receive. Consider:

1. The easier you make it for someone to give you feedback, the greater the volume of data collection will be.
2. A question with limited responses one can identify works best.
3. A question with a fill in the blank response gets the second-best response.
4. A question with an open ended narrative space gets the least amount of response.
5. If you want the hard document back, provide a return envelope and postage pre-paid.
6. You can use on-line portals that market, administrate and facilitate surveys; There are a lot of on-line vendor options available for use or tie-in use with your CRM/Database systems.
7. When you are with a group of profile prospects or clients, it's a great time to ask for feedback on things you are doing or considering, or to ask open-ended questions on how to better engage the marketplace.

Most sales professionals and sales organizations do not make survey-speak a part of their regular marketplace interactions and instead, treat survey work is a special stand-alone endeavor done formally once a year. This is a missed opportunity to sell more, sell better and attract new business opportunities.

Chapter 63

Performance Driven Selling©
Telephone Power & Using PIE™
to Master the Telephone

The reality of selling and business development, is that in order to grow, you need more new business or your need more business from your existing clients. In every selling profession, reaching the unknown market can be done in many ways: Internet marketing, social media, hard lead generation, referrals and recommendations, advertising, awareness campaigns, media, engaged COIs, networking, face-to-face area canvassing, trade/exhibit show booths, internal campaigns from existing clients/members to generate qualified leads, and... making phone calls.

Businesses can automate the calling campaigns for the sales team, CRMs can be designed to systematize outbound calls for sales professionals to keep them on the phone and outbound call centers can be engaged. But, at the end of the day it is the responsibility of the professional sales person to own their market and all the strategic and tactical responsibilities associated with that book of business.

No matter what your business, every successful selling professional has some degree of new lead flow into their Sales Funnel/Pipeline™ on a regular basis – phone calls. My work with the largest Real Estate Firms in America demonstrates that one hour minimum daily for new listing is the start of their Sales Funnel/Pipeline™. For the Pharmaceutical industry 10 to 12 doctor office visits each day, feeds their Sales Funnel/Pipeline™. The Financial Services industry benchmarks off of a set number of new outbound calls made and contacts reached each day for their Sales Funnel/Pipeline™ for new associates until their portfolio is built.

I worked with Military Recruiters for more than two decades, consistently exceeding mission, because they maintained a daily routine of new outbound calls each day to meet and have a substantive conversation with five new people daily to feed their Sales Funnel/Pipeline™. This a total of 1,825 new contacts annually. For individuals in the professional services industry, PIE™ is the secret to success (more on this formula later).

Successful sales professionals recognize that the telephone is an instrument or tool for success attainment. The number of contacts that can be made via the telephone is significantly greater than from actual face-to-face contacts.

Most sales professionals shy away from using the telephone as a strategic instrument that can be used to increase Suspect and Prospect contact. Most sales professionals, they would prefer to use the telephone for visiting rather than selling. Others tend to shy away from using the telephone as a way to maximize selling time and avoid using the telephone for the majority of the day – untrained sales professionals hate cold calling and tend to see the telephone as the instrument of death always associated with that process.

Turn "Cold Calling" into "Warm Calling" with a simple adjustment in your mindset and your use of technology.

1. If you have a new name and their email, you can create a simple email to send prior to calling. Then whether you reach the person live or their voice mail, you can start the conversation with a reference to the email you sent.

2. Send them a value-based message with a powerful WHY that you want to talk to them, send this 24-to-48 hours in advance.

3. In the email make it easy for them to see your call back phone number in case your message is so compelling to them that they are motivated to call you before you can call them.

4. I would tee-up 25 to 50 new people each week to call, send them an email on Monday/Tuesday (i.e. defer to *Rule 1-52-X*™) and thus holding yourself accountable to call them then on Tuesday-Wednesday-Thursday for discussion, appointment setting, etc.

Sales professional must recognize that the telephone should be used to maximize selling associated activities and a means to really maximizing time. Use the telephone to:

1. Reach out and introduce yourself and your offers

2. Call people that have been referred to you by clients and "Advocates"

3. Follow-up with happy customers for additional opportunities during down time and non-presentation times

4. Have the names and cell phone numbers of all hot leads in your phone contacts list, so in between meetings and in awkward idle minutes you can call or text for connectivity

5. Establish meeting times with Prospects and Customers

6. Close sales

7. Reach out and make those return calls of low importance during down times or times when you can be multi-tasking

8. After hours to reach out and make significantly more calls (if the sole intent is to leave action-oriented information packed voicemail messages)

9. During what may be prime calling time to reach others when they are least likely to have gate-keepers at their site

10. To make short cycle contacts when you need to connect with someone for a specific situational agenda. Make that connection and then terminate your call

As sales professionals, take a look at the high yielding contact times and low contact times, and then coordinate your schedules accordingly. For example, if Monday mornings are difficult to reach contacts (for whatever reason), then don't plan for Monday mornings to be heavy outbound calling times. If you keep a contact log (diary, database management system, personal calendar) with notations of individuals that have been talked to earlier and whom have requested a follow-up on a specific date and time, then over-coming call resistance is easily attained – now you have set calls to be made for a purpose.

Most sales professionals suck at making outbound sales calls and can rattle off an endless list of "reasons" for not making outbound calls. However, there is always a statistical correlation between:

1. How many times you dial. *Think of this as feeding the top your Sales Funnel/Pipeline™,*

2. How many times you dial and leave a message. *Think of this as feeding the top your Sales Funnel/Pipeline™.*

3. How many times you dial, leave a message or reach a gate-keeper and then actually connect with your target prospect or customer. *Think of this as pulling the lead from the top down into the middle of your Sales Funnel/Pipeline™.*

4. How many times you have to dial and connect before you get a face-to-face or phone presentation opportunity. *Think of this as pulling the lead from the top down into the middle of your Sales Funnel/Pipeline™.*

5. How many opportunities to present and determining how many times you actually convert all those calls into a new sale. *Think of this as pulling the lead from the top down into the middle as a contact and now down and out of the bottom of your Sales Funnel/Pipeline™.*

Using the dashboard analytics you have in your reporting system, if these five obvious data points are not easily ascertained, then take a piece of paper for one week and make your own home-grown manual tracking form. Make a check mark under how many times you dial in any one day. A check mark for left message, a check mark for talked to someone live and left a message, check mark for actually talked to contact, check mark under proposal made or sent. Now you can see at the end of any day how many dials you actually made and how many of those dials it took to generate meaningful interaction. The drill here is to determine your *"Magic Number."* Wouldn't it be nice to know that for you it takes ten dials to get one solid contact, and it takes ten proposals to get one new client. This would tell you how many dials you need to make every day to be successful.

A common frustration for sales professionals is leaving or receiving telephone messages that seem vague and don't provide a next step. When you leave a message for someone else (whether it is in an electronic voice system or with an actual person at the other end of the telephone), make sure that your message is action oriented. Consider:

1. Leave your name, spell it.
2. Leave your telephone number for follow-up, repeat it twice.
3. Leave an action-oriented message that tells the listener exactly what you want them to do.
4. Your message must have a significant value to the listener that indicates to them that by calling you back you can make their life better

If you are leaving a message with an actual person at the other end, before you do any of the above four items, start by politely asking the other person, **"do you have something to write with and on?"**

WOW. You will be amazed how many times the other person will say, "Just a moment. Let me get something." The sales person was about to leave a message with someone, who in actuality was not writing anything down.

If you leave the message in someone's electronic voicemail system, consider standing up as you leave the message. This change in physiology makes your voice sound significantly firmer, solid and more energized.

Just as with face-to-face interactions, remember that you should always have a purpose for a conversation (Remember, "Stacking-N-Linking™" previously presented in this book?) The telephone is an interruption in the other person's life (unless they specifically requested that you call them), so the conversation must have a purpose and once accomplished don't violate that purpose by continuing.

To maximize over-all sales activities, monitor your own daily activities and account development activities to recognize what times during each day are best times to place and receive calls, consider working across time zones if applicable and how that can allow you to maximize your over-all daily productivity.

Recognize that your ability to cultivate relationships with people over the telephone is essential for sales transactions. Getting the "gate-keeper" at the other end to accept you may make the difference in getting through to the intended contact or merely leaving endless messages. Knowing others voicemail system extension numbers allows the sales professional to reach out and leave action-oriented messages before and after traditional work hours.

With the telephone, ensure that you use it to peak performance, arming yourself with reference materials, files, computer access, work space, etc., within reach. If you need a cordless phone, a longer receiver cord, a headset, a cellular phone, etc., then buy it, even if your organization won't.

Like it or not, the telephone is a powerful selling tool through which relationships can be fast-tracked and greater levels of efficiency attained.

For solo-practitioners or professional services providers, I recommend using the *PIE*™ formula when face-to-face selling is not possible.

1. "P" is for Phone calls made outbound, as discussed above.

2. "I" is for phone Interviews engaged in or discussions with qualified conversations, where you explore the other persons needs and your ability to provide meaningful solutions to them.

3. "E" is for Emails with hyper-links to your website, social media, or attachments that represent a next step in the sales phone conversation whereby you have sent them a proposal, application, documents, etc., that

moves the person from Suspect to Prospect to Qualified Contact in route to becoming your next customer/client/enlistment to your Sales Funnel/Pipeline™.

Just as with any lead flow analysis, you want to reverse track each sale to determine how many conversations you must have, and from those finite number of prospect conversations, how many people in general (Leads) did you have to connect with? This again, becomes your "Magic Number" and every successful sales professional has a general if not very specific number in their head for each phase through the Sales Funnel/Pipeline™ from top to bottom. Do you know your "Magic Number"?

If you are a professional sales representative/recruiter, in order to grow you need more new business or your need more business from your existing clients. This means you need to be where the market is and where the market will be – the phone is your power tool.

Chapter 64

Performance Driven Selling©
Using Your Business Card as
Your #1 Selling Instrument

CAUTION: In some industries, the following ideas may be legislated by law or policy. Use common sense when deploying these ideas. When you cannot do a specific tactical below, understand the strategic point and then look for ways to accomplish the bigger picture, which is to make sure your business cards do not collect dust in your supply box.

The easiest, most inexpensive branding tool you can use in the face-to-face world of interpersonal relationships, is the business card. It is our silent salesman and your card establishes who you are to others. Great sales professionals never miss a networking opportunity.

The business card is to a sales professional as road sign are along the highways of life. It tells people who you are and how to reach you. Successful sales professionals know that you never know when a great selling opportunity may present itself and having a business card to offer someone can really make you stand out.

The size, shape, feel, colors, words, titles, contact options, etc. are important. Business cards are also a powerful way to determine if you are investing enough time with Suspects and Prospects in the Sales Pipeline Funnel. When you are truly in a sales position, then getting your card into the right hand is critical, as is following up with the cards you've received. Warehousing business cards in ones' desk drawer is a sign of lack of work rather than a sign of smart work.

Whether you are a super sales star, a sales trainer, sales manager or business owner, you can track the amount of business cards and frequency of re-orders to determine how often you prospect and connect with the marketplace.

There are many ways in which a business card can be used to bring greater value to the recipient and yield greater returns for the sales professional. Consider:

1. As most business cards are blank on the reverse side or have ample blank space, this is a great place to make specific notations for the prospect or customer on special Feature/Benefit items that you are offering to them. Research indicates that people are more inclined to keep your business card and more inclined to discard the brochures and handouts that sales professionals tend to load them down with. *(If you are in an industry where personalizing like this would be against the law, have key product or product data on the reverse)*

2. A powerful way to use the business card as a customized selling brochure is to draw a small circle on the blank side about the size of a small coin. Inside the circle, write their Name and date within the circle representing when you made the following notes and gave them card. Then for any key presentation point, fact/feature item, major offer, price, benefit, etc., that relates to that encircled notation, draw simple, short axis lines outward from the circle and write that simple notation on each line.

You'll be giving them a special, customized print reference instrument; a MindMap™ in essence.

1. You can use the business card as a means of soliciting someone's name and title by offering your card to the other person at the beginning of the sales conversation and requesting theirs. Then take their card and leave it out in front of you during your sales

conversation/presentation, so that at any time if you forget the other person's name(s), you can cheat and look down at the card and maintain conversation flow and control.

2. You can offer an extra card to any prospect at the moment they become a happy customer, as a means of involving them as a referral agent or COI for you. Example: *"Here's an extra card for you, should you know of someone that would be appropriate to benefit from this product/service as you have. Thank you."*

3. In any follow-up letters, "Thank You" letters or introduction prospecting letters, such as in the deployment of Rule 1-52-X™, you can always include a few cards, one for the intended reader and extras for them to pass along to others.

4. Place the business card in "Give-Away" drawing bowls/jars on counters in stores with high volume pedestrian traffic of your "profile" prospects and customers. Position it to face outward so it serves as a free billboard until the drawing date.

5. Look for display areas where your business card can be "thumb tacked" up when and where appropriate, included in other merchant's direct mail circulars/envelopes/mail packs, etc., magnetized a hung-up, used as a book mark or other multipurpose instrument.

6. You can post the card onto electronic social media walls, paid print promotional or advertising spaces.

7. Ask other, "if you were the intended profile target to receive my card, what information would you want to have access to?" Then make sure that information is on your card. You can always submit your prototype card

to a sampling of trusted advisors and clients before you finalize them and produce them for feedback.

8. You can produce special print runs of your business cards and on the reverse side of the card leverage that space as valuable real estate and provide customized information for a special meeting you are attending or presentation you are giving, or for client centric information.

   a. I've used this as a powerful take-away tool in my Keynotes and Training Programs for decades. On the reverse of my business card I print a mini handout of key take away action points from my talks. Attendees and meeting planners have raved about this value-added touch every time.

   b. If you were attending a Trade Show you could have special exhibit information on the reverse or special deals being offered there or helpful tips for that event of general interest to people. This provides more utility in your card at the venue and time and increases the odds of people wanting, keeping and referring to your card, all the while with your contact data on the front.

   c. I have coached military Recruiters to produce special runs of local community events on the reverse of their cards for small-town-America and suburbia, print high school athletic schedules on the reverse, county/state fair schedules, etc., again a service touch-point of providing valuable information that their market would want and all the while their contact data is on the front of every card carried.

Get creative about other ways to use the traditional calling card to raise your brand in the marketplace and generate more business selling opportunities. Always ask yourself, if you chose to have a professional card, what is the intended use and who are the intended recipients? "You never get a second chance to make a first impression," so make your card appropriate and not foolish and silly... unless that is what you are selling.

As a sales professional, recognize that there are a lot of powerful ways to utilize your business card as a powerful selling instrument. I order 1,000 cards at a time and then rubber band them in counts of 250-cards (bricks) each. I monitor how often I am making new connections, by how many bricks I am moving or not. The cards sent out are like seeds, the more seeds that one plants, the greater their potential harvests.

Chapter 65

Performance Driven Selling®
Advancing the Involved Sale
Forward in Your Sales
Pipeline/Funnel with
"Call to Action" (CTA) Next Steps

Most sales are not one-and-done interactions, there are multiple steps to accomplish throughout the sales process which may require multiple re-engagement or follow-up interactions. The more interactions necessary to make a sale, the more difficult it may become to re-connect with your prospect and nail down for that final sale.

The art and science of moving forward is to ensure you get the next call-back meeting secured by gaining "buy-in" from your prospect or client with a clear, concise, next action step commitment – a *Call to Action*.

Each step of the five-step selling process we've discussed in this book may involve an individual, smaller sale. The next action step should be measurable and easy for everyone involved to understand and accomplish. This will allow you to generate and maintain forward momentum all along the consultative selling process. In essence, what you may be selling at each step, is not the end-game or ultimate sale or commitment, it may be that you are selling and closing the other party on the next action step necessary to continue forward towards that ultimate final sale.

With each interaction, make sure you get confirmation and commitment to the next action step. Examples:

1. *If you are selling an involved purchase,* there may be necessary documents at certain stages of an application process. Getting each of these may be the next step and if not continuously sold, the other party can become frustrated or discouraged. This becomes an opportunity for them to un-sell themselves on you and the offer.

2. *If you are recruiting someone to your organization,* there may be multiple vetting steps along the way or situations may develop that require additional documentation. Make sure that you keep the other party excited and engaged and sell them on each next step. Do not give them any reason to become discouraged or negative, as that will become an un-selling point in their mind. If possible, keep them engaged in the next action step by having them proactively gather information, with deadlines, so you can continue the forward progress. If you are more excited to recruit them, than they are to join you, you are selling against a lot of potential complacency and negative energy from the side of the prospect. Make sure you are continuously selling and closing them throughout the process.

3. *If you are selling to a committee or multiple decision makers,* be prepared and excited for the opportunity to engage multiple participants. If you deliver solutions to them and forge that selling relationship, you may create multiple COIs for what you do. As you identify the buying roles each serve, you become more versed in your deliverables and may find yourself making multiple selling points and closing on multiple needs for

each party involved. Just as you would do in any involved selling/presenting process, make sure you identify the next action steps with these participants, get buy-in and confirmation on the next selling step, and identify (with their agreement) what happens after that step. Keep everyone forward focused and not overwhelmed.

You must be consistently moving the contact through your selling pipeline/funnel process — from contact to contract. If you know that there is a typical sequence in your selling cycle, you might consider creating a flow document as you start the process. This will show them that there are several check-points of what you and they will be doing along the selling-closing process.

4. *Maintain Forward Momentum with Leveraged Connections* – The time in between your connections are opportunities for the prospect or customer to stop-out of the selling process. A great way to combat this is to sequence additional added-value reinforcement messaging for your potential customer/recruit. Make this an intermittingly sequenced campaign from the first point of slow-down in the selling funnel/pipeline sequence, all the way through to the closure point.

Stay focused on the other person's most critical need that your offer will resolve and subtly reinforce it with each forward momentum leveraged connection that you draw upon. You could have:

1. Reinforcement endorsement letter or message from a client that fits the Profile of the prospect you are working with, that you mail to them, a sort of a drip campaign

2. Reinforcement endorsement message from a client that fits the Profile of the prospect you are working with, that

you send to them on their social media platforms, a sort of a drip campaign

3. Reinforcement endorsement message from you or a client that fits the Profile of the prospect you are working with, to them as a text message, a sort of a drip campaign

4. Reinforcement endorsement letter or message from another member of your organization, that addresses perceived anxiety in the selling process that they might have, a sort of a drip campaign

5. Reinforcement endorsement letter or message from another member of your organization that they would know and respect, that addresses perceived anxiety or questions in the selling process that they might have, a sort of a friendly drip campaign

6. Reinforcement endorsement letter or message from your "boss" to the prospect you are working with, welcoming them to the process and thanking them for what they are about to do, a sort of a drip campaign

5. *Call-to-Action Next Sequential Step* - If the next step if for you to produce documents or information to send to the client by x-date and x-time, make sure you get a commitment right then as to when you will talk next and what that next action step will be at that time.

This allows you to not only ensure forward progression, it also serves as a conversational vetting opportunity to ensure that you have and are continuously qualifying the prospect or customer and thus determine that they are serious about the next action step. Watch their body language and assess their responses to ensure they are in alignment with the agreed upon next action step. If you sense hesitancy, now is the time for further conversation to ensure you are not being led down an ultimate no-sale lane.

Additionally, a few easy professional follow-up and engagement strategies may be to send an email, social media message or text prior to your next call or meeting, *"Trust you are doing great, just confirming our call in 30-minutes..."* or *""Trust you are doing great, just confirming our meeting tomorrow at ..."* This simple strategy has served me well by keeping everyone focused and moving forward throughout the interactions.

Remember, most sales are not "one and done" transactions and the more interactions necessary to make a sale complete, the more opportunities to lose the sale. By making mini sales and closes along the way, you can work against losing connection with the party.

Stay focused and remember that most selling professionals stop engaging and working to make a sale after the third to fourth interaction or attempted contact, even though most sales actually take place on or after the fifth meaningful interaction.

Advancing the involved sale forward may mean multiple mini sales and clearly defined *Call-to-Actions*.

Chapter 66

Performance Driven Selling©
Your MORGUE & Cleaning
Up Lost POCs & Inactive
Clients for ROI

Another great place to mine for business opportunities and sometimes missed 'low hanging fruit', is in your own backyard. In every organization and CRM, there are valuable sales just waiting to be made. Unfortunately, everyone has either discounted, dismissed or in some cases not even realized what gold mine selling opportunities are already sitting dormant within your organization and past sales colleagues' files.

When I was just entering my professional selling career, I worked in an organization that had a room off the lobby. Inside, were a row of beautiful filing cabinets with hard copies of folders, from A-Z. One day I asked the owner what that room was, and he jokingly referred to it as the "morgue".

"What do you mean?"

"That is the room of files of inactive and past clients that we no longer do business with."

My mental marketing wheels started churning, I recognized that while I personally knew none of those contacts, they did not know me either. Consider these thoughts when performing this post-mortem analysis of the accounts in your morgue:

1. If they left for *personality fallout* issues with a previous professional colleague within this organization, I am not them. And if we have a legitimate solution that could help them, I am a new name and face, then I owe it to them to at least make them aware of this

2. If they left for *legitimate product deliverable reasons*, and if we have a legitimate solution that could help them, then I owe it to them to at least make them aware of this

3. If they left due to *financial reasons*, then maybe those can be re-discussed and perhaps any issues on their end have been resolved, and if we have a legitimate solution that could help them, then I owe it to them to at least make them aware of this

4. If they left due to *timing reasons*, then maybe those can be re-discussed and perhaps any issues on their end have been resolved, and if we have a legitimate solution that could help them, then I owe it to them to at least make them aware of this

5. If they *did not become a client because our organization or my predecessor dropped the ball at our end*, then maybe those can be re-discussed, and if we have a legitimate solution that could help them, then I owe it to them to at least make them aware of this

6. If they *did not become a client because they decided to go with my competition*, then maybe a courtesy check-in with them may reveal that their needs are not being met and we may be a viable option for them to transition to now or in the near future. I owe it to them to at least make them aware of this

7. If they *did not become a client because they decided to do nothing at the time*, then maybe a courtesy check-in with them may reveal that their needs are now different and my deliverables may be exactly what they need today. And, if we have a legitimate solution that could help them, then I owe it to them to at least make them aware of this

In every organization there is a morgue, whether on-line or in file cabinets, with accounts and leads that everyone believes are dead. These missed selling opportunities can be your gold mine. The valuable lost leads, inactive clients and dead proposals/contracts/bids/applications that can be or may be able to be resurrected could be your next sales win.

The massive amount of lost energy and expenses associated with getting a selling professional up-to-speed and then having them leave, is staggering. Along with this, is the possible number of warm and hot leads that selling professional might have been working at the time they left, and in most organizations, there is no effective way of capturing that data and following up with these contacts. Make it a side-bar endeavor to reflect on who was calling on your market before you and before them as there may be great leads sitting dormant in the morgue.

Add these contacts into your awareness campaigns, invite them to appropriate on-line and live events. Consider your touch-points to active clients/members to your organization, and how you would be courting a great prospect today, and consider enrolling these new contacts accordingly as well.

Through this reconnection campaign, you may be rebuilding goodwill, uncovering new selling opportunities, reactivating lost COIs and accelerating your market dominance.

Chapter 67

Performance Driven Selling©
LeadGenerator™ & Target Rich
Environment (TRE) Analytics
Tell You Where the Market Is
Now and Tomorrow

A professional salesperson has a never-ending passion to ensure that everyone in your market that can benefit from what you have to offer, know what you have to offer.

Understanding the analytics of quality lead generation and lead flow for today's sale and tomorrow's sale, is critical on the frontline and in the boardroom. You must be able to recognize the market or areas from which you tend to do the majority of your work and receive the majority of your business leads, referrals, connections and sales. This highly productive contact base is known as your Target-Rich Environment (TRE). To increase sales effectiveness, first identify your TRE: Clients from an area that provides more business, clients with whom you have a great affinity, and clients who are naturally easier to work with.

Most sales professionals don't recognize that they tend to lean their activities in specific directions or sell into specific areas. By identifying this trend activity, a sales professional's first responsibility is to ensure that he or she is thoroughly working the TREs every day. As an example, a sales professional's perspective can be limited to just the larger, more well-known businesses or lead source contact areas within that TRE or within the salesperson's geographical region. To increase this awareness, benchmark what a great Avatar for you looks like (whether to your organization or to a specific offering you have or need) and identify where you are finding these sales now and where you tend to go to make these sales – that is your existing TRE.

By recognizing the greatest lead sources for what you have to offer, you can begin to grow your business opportunities. For help in recognizing these greatest lead areas, recognize all of the "present tense" answers from where you presently make your sales. First, create a comprehensive list of successful sales transactions. For example, list the actual buyers of a single offer you have made. When that list is complete and you recognize that this is in fact a finite list, then push yourself by asking, "If I could no longer market or sell to these identified contacts, who else would be candidates for what I have to offer?" This second question is the starting point for finding more business opportunities.

I have done this exercise and accelerated sales ROI within the pharma industry, automotive and motorcycle industry, at the retail level, construction, manufacturing, consumer products, hi-tech, financial services, real estate, direct marketing, on-line, etc., and it always works.

Here is an example from one of my clients, the National Guard recruiting sales forces across America. This TRE strategy, aligned with our other professional development protocols have been used by States to move from last place to first place within 16-months or less, and you can do it too. For two-decades I tracked data with the top Recruiters nationally. Most recruiters that struggle to make their sales goals work twenty or fewer regular TRE lead sources. By looking at present tense v. future tense TRE methodologies, you can increase your TRE lead source by an X-Factor that will actually overwhelm your abilities – I call the modeling exercise the LeadGenerator™ system.

This LeadGenerator™ lists more than 250 TREs that the sales/recruiter is directed to use the list as a reference chart, eliminating all of the TREs that are truly not applicable for his or her demographic and geography, checking off those presently being worked, and recognizing the net opportunities left for quality lead generation efforts . . . thereby feeding one's sales activity funnel.

Quick-Reference Lead Generator for National GUARD Recruiting (template example)

Quick-Reference Lead Generator Example:

Step One: Start with the last person you recruited, identify where you connected with them in your marketplace... that is their TRE. Now, ask him or her for at least three referrals. This is possibly a list of new TREs. Next, get a roster of every member of your current unit, company and identify the limited few that can understand and reflect your Avatar and ask each one for referrals every month.

Step Two: Consider each TRE™ as Rule 1-52-X™ targets for regular mailers, e-mails, marketing, direct mailings, promotions, advertising, circulars, brochures, PDFs, Website marketing, blogs, gifting, social media connectivity, etc.

Step Three: Regularly contact, visit, share leads with, and make sure all other area service recruiters know about you.

Step Four: Read each of the following for additional market ideas.

ARNG Primary Market (17-21):

COACHES (Male/Female as appropriate):

1. Review student newspaper or guidance office roster for where graduating students are listed to be going or not going upon graduation!!!!!!!!!!
2. Basketball
3. Baseball
4. Wrestling
5. Track
6. Cross Country
7. Volleyball
8. Swimming
9. Football
10. Tennis
11. Lacrosse
12. Hockey
13. Golf
14. Gymnastics
15. Cheer/Yell
16. Team Captain's
17. Team Leader's ... and their friends
18. Etc.
19. Volunteer to be an assistant coach yourself

On-Campus & Extra Curricular Sponsors/Locations:

1. Regularly review school website updates and school social media posts for real time highlights of outstanding students for your follow-up
2. Leadership Program(s) Advisors
3. FFA – Future Farmers of America AgEd Teacher
4. FFA – AgEd Advisor
5. FFA Chapter members
6. Professional Speakers that speak to different Affinity Groups on a Campus or Associations from a Campus that meet off campus (i.e. NSA / NationalSpeakersAssociation.org search for speakers that speak to HS/Collegiate audiences, make them aware of your Deliverables as a regular COI connection!)
7. Library

8. Classrooms
9. Newspaper
10. Yearbook
11. Votech
12. Shop
13. Drama
14. Band
15. Choir
16. Peer Support Groups
17. Youth Group/Ministry Groups
18. Student Government
19. Ball Fields a. Baseball b. Soccer c. Football d. Etc.
20. Sports Courts
21. Skateboard Parks
22. On Campus Walking Around/Sitting
23. Recreation Centers
24. Cafeteria's
25. Driver's Education
26. 4-H
27. NYFEA
28. DECA
29. VICA
30. Blue Key
31. Military Academy Applicant's
32. Jr. ROTC
33. Early admittance Military Academy bound students
34. Principal
35. Administrators
36. Head Master
37. Librarian
38. Foreign Language Teacher's
39. Guidance Counselor's
40. Career Counselor's
41. AP/Honors Classes/Instructors
42. Custodian/Campus Employee Lead Referrals
43. Campus Security Employee Lead referrals
44. Dungeons & Dragons
45. Chess
46. PTA

47. Nurses Offices
48. Parking Lot
49. Parent and Teachers Association
50. Boys State
51. Girls State
52. Monthly, Quarterly, Annual (Fall &/or Spring Banquets) Awards on-campus events by "affinity group" like Sports, Academic, FFA, etc.
53. Etc.

Community Contact Locations:

1. Consider every option below as 24/7 TREs, where do all of these leads work/live from 11PM-7AM
2. www.Facebook.com
3. Instagram
4. www.Teens4Hire.org
5. ORPHAN Adoption Selling/Marketing
6. Become a Boys/Girls Club Mentor/Ambassador
7. Fitness Center Trainers/Coaches as COIs
8. Hair Solon Stylists as COIs
9. Martial Art Studios
10. Gas Stations
11. GED Test Prep Sites & Test Sites
12. Movie Theaters
13. Paint Ball Camps/Facilities
14. Restaurants (dine in and sit down)
15. Restaurants (Fast Food eateries)
16. Restaurant Delivery Drivers
17. Restaurants (Pizza Shops) after Games
18. Church Youth Groups
19. Motor Vehicle Records
20. Pool Halls
21. Bowling Alleys
22. Community Centers
23. Job Corp Centers
24. Car Washes
25. Seasonal Employer's
26. Ball Fields

27. Parks
28. Driving their vehicle's and parking at teen hangouts
29. Job Fairs
30. College Fairs
31. County Fair
32. Concerts
33. Golf Courses
34. Hotels
35. Airports
36. Bus Stations
37. Train Stations
38. Baby Sitters
39. Internet Chat Rooms
40. Internet Website Postings
41. Search Engine Postings
42. Grain Elevator
43. Shopping Mall
44. Food Courts
45. Employment Agencies
 46. Sylvan Learning Centers
47. Kaplan Learning Centers
48. Princeton Review Learning Center
49. Book Stores
50. Magazine Stands-Racks-Stores
51. Grocery Stores
52. Video Arcades
53. Video Rental Centers
54. Music Stores
55. On the Bus, Bus Station
56. Valets
57. Leads from EVERY immediate enlistment ... their friends, family members, etc.
58. Two Year College/Community Recruiters
59. Four Year College Recruiters
60. Trade School Administrators/Owners
61. Trade School Admission Counselors
62. Certification Processors
63. Apprentice/Trade Association
64. Concerts/Vendor Booth's

65. Bank
66. Auto repair shops
67. Community late night hangouts (where teens gather in warm weather season on Friday and Saturday nights for example...)
68. Parades
69. Baby sitters
70. Family members
71. Friends
72. Friends network of people they know
73. Neighbors
74. Coffee Houses
75. 1-800-Go-Guard leads
76. NGB Leads
77. ASVAB list
78. Farms
79. Fleet
80. Factories
81. Armory / Drill / PT / Member Inquiries for leads...
82. Civic volunteering
83. Exhibit areas
84. Warrior Challenge
85. Civic area 10Ks, half-marathons, marathons, Ironman competitions, etc.
86. Facebook Sites
87. Facebook – Friends Surfing
88. Facebook – Likes
89. Facebook Banner Ads
90. All on-line social media platforms
91. Etc.

POST H.S. / Commencement Lead TREs!!!!!

1. Get final year student newspaper or Counselor log detailing where everyone is or is not going upon graduation – send Congratulations Letter and Call COI's for updates to work...

ARNG Secondary Market – College/Post College Age 18- 28 Market: P COACHES (Male/Female as appropriate):

1. Basketball
2. Baseball
3. Wrestling
4. Track
5. Cross Country
6. Volleyball
7. Swimming
8. Football
9. Tennis
10. Hockey
11. Golf
12. Lacrosse
13. Gymnastics
14. Team Captain's
15. Team Leader's ... and their friends
16. Etc.

On-Campus & Extra Curricular Sponsors/Locations:

1. Regularly review school website updates and school social media posts for real time highlights of outstanding students for your follow-up
2. Library
3. Classrooms
4. Newspaper
5. Yearbook
6. Radio/Television Outlets-Facilities
7. Fraternities
8. Sororities
9. IFC
10. PanHellenic
11. Votech
12. Shop/Craft Facilities
13. Drama
14. Band
15. Choir
16. Peer Support Groups
17. Student Government
18. Ball Fields

19. Sports Courts
20. On Campus
21. Recreation Centers
22. Cafeteria's
23. Pool Hall
24. Bars
25. Clubs
26. Campus Financial Aid representatives
27. Campus Book Store
28. Campus Student Union
29. Campus Community Center
30. Campus Sports Center
31. ROTC Center/Military Sciences
32. Drill Weekend Friends/Guests
33. Campus VA Office
34. NYFEA
35. Guidance Counselor's
36. Career Counselor's
37. Class/Major Advisor
38. Dorms
39. Snack Court / Cafeteria/ Cyber-Cafe
40. Etc.

Community Contact Locations:

1. Consider every option below as 24/7 TREs, where do all of these leads work/live from 11PM-7AM
2. LinkedIn.com
3. Facebook.com
4. Instagram
5. All on-line social media platforms & job wanted/search sections
6. All on-line service bureau platforms & job wanted/search sections
7. Job Aggregators (on-line career sites)
8. Your Website, multiple entry points
9. US Jayce's Chapter's
10. Kiwanis
11. Rotary

12. Community Civic service groups
13. Wedding Announcements
14. Baby announcements to parents
15. Hotel, Meeting, Conference venue locations lists of upcoming meetings that you could have an informational table/booth at
16. www.Facebook.com
17. Help Wanted or Things for sale community bulletin boards where you can place signage
18. FFA-AA – Future Farmers Of America Alumni Affiliate Group
19. ORPHAN Adoption Selling/Marketing
20. Bankruptcy Court Records
21. Government Job Search, Jobs Corp & Employment Services Agencies
22. Local COMMERCIAL Job Search & Employment Services Company or Franchise
23. Cash Advance/Money Stores/Kiosks – post your S posters & job opportunities posters
24. Gas Stations
25. Move Theaters
26. Ski Clubs
27. Climbing Clubs
28. Gun Clubs
29. Gym memberships
30. Cross-Fit Groups
31. Newspapers of People Profiled
32. Restaurants (dine in and sit down)
33. Restaurants (Fast Food eateries)
34. Restaurant Delivery Drivers
35. Church Youth Groups
36. Motor Vehicle Records
37. Pool Halls
38. Marksmanship Clubs
39. Athletic and Health Cubs
40. Bowling Alleys
41. Community Centers
42. Job Corp Centers
43. Car Washes

44. Seasonal Employer's
45. Ball Fields
46. Parks
47. Driving their vehicle's and parking at teen hangouts
48. Job Fairs
49. County Fair
50. Concerts
51. Golf Courses
52. Hotels
53. Airports
54. Bus Stations
55. Train Stations
56. Internet Chat Rooms
57. Internet Website Postings
58. Search Engine Postings
59. Grain Elevator
60. Shopping Mall
61. Food Courts
62. Employment Agencies
63. Learning Centers (Sylvan, etc.)
64. Book Stores
65. Magazine Racks
66. Grocery Stores
67. Video Arcades
68. Video Rental Centers
69. On the Bus
70. Valets
71. Leads from EVERY immediate enlistment ... their friends, family members, etc.
72. Two Year College/Community Recruiters
73. Four Year College Recruiters
74. Concerts/Vendor Booth's
75. Banks
76. Auto Teller machines
77. Auto stores
78. Laundry Mat
79. Late night eateries
80. Job career centers / work force centers

81. Other military service Recruiters offices, fairs, booths, display areas

82. Community late night hangouts (where teens gather in warm weather season on Friday and Saturday nights for example...)

83. Parades

84. Recent enlistments

85. Baby sitters

86. Family members

87. Friends

88. Friends network of people they know

89. Neighbors 90. Coffee houses

91. Campus area apartment complexes (mailrooms, bulletin boards, offices, car windows, etc...)

92. YMCA

93. Camp grounds

94. 1-800-Go-Guard leads

95. NGB Leads

96. ASVAB list

97. Farms

98. Fleet

99. Factories

100. Armory

101. Civic volunteering

102. Exhibit areas

103. Casino

104. Business/Factory closing outplacement informational exposure

105. Police Training Academy

106. Fire Training Academy

107. EMS

108. Review year-end student newspaper or guidance office roster for where graduating students are listed to be going or not going upon graduation!!!!!!!!!!

109. All LOCAL/MUNICIPAL government employees (pre-vetted)

110. All COUNTY government employees (pre-vetted)

111. All STATE government employees (pre-vetted)

112. All FEDERAL government employees in your area (pre-vetted)

113. Bankruptcy Court Records

114. Government Job Search, Jobs Corp & Employment Services Agencies

115. Local COMMERCIAL Job Search & Employment Services Company or Franchise

116. Etc.

ARNG Tertiary Market – Age 28-35 & Under Market:

1. Consider every option below as 24/7 TREs, where do all of these leads work/live from 11PM-7AM

2. All LOCAL/MUNICIPAL government employees (pre-vetted)

3. All COUNTY government employees (pre-vetted)

4. All STATE government employees (pre-vetted)

5. All FEDERAL government employees in your area (pre-vetted)

6. Chamber of Commerce in mid to large metros have YP (Young Professional) groups

7. All First Responders, are pre-vetted for you and if between 25-35 years of age great POCs to share how the Guard can accelerate their career success and value to their market place

8. All Government Agencies/Employers a. City Agencies/Government b. County Agencies/Government c. State Agencies/Government d. Federal Agencies/Government e. Veterans Agencies/Government

9. Make sure you have real-time updates of individuals that have gotten out of the Service in past 3-years, and connect with each for reality check of their life today and interest in reenlisting?

10. All on-line social media platforms

11. All on-line service bureau platforms a. All Job Search platforms

12. Job Aggregators (on-line career sites)

13. All local community employment search firms, agencies, coordinators

14. Your Website, multiple entry points

15. US Jaycee's Chapter's

16. Any Career Fair, Job Fair, Employment Fair expos ... a. Sponsored by local Radio Stations b. "" Televisions Stations c.

"" Print Media d. "" Employment Search Firms e. "" Job Services Agencies f. "" Church's g. "" etc.

17. Municipal Airport is a municipality into itself ... a. all ground tarmac employees b. emergency services staff c. infrastructure employees d. individual airlines station employees e. customer service merchant providers f. etc. personnel

18. Hair Salon/Barber Shop Employee as COI

19. Young Professional / TYPros Groups

20. LinkedIn

21. Facebook

22. Craigslist

23. Phonebook

24. Courthouse – Prior Service file their DD214 in their local court houses; Check logs regularly...

25. Drivers license records

26. Job Corps Centers

27. ExpressServices

28. Robert Half & Associates

29. Consumer Credit Counseling Centers

30. Review local newspapers and trade association newsletter regularly for their meetings and networking opportunities to attend, showcase, present, exhibit, etc.

31. Id if there is a local Young Professionals (YPros) Chapter associated with your local (metro typically) Chamber-of-Commerce to associate within

32. Id area Chapter's of the United States Junior Chamber (USJaycees) to explore for membership affiliation, strategic alliance partnerships, or recruitment opportunities

33. Rotary

34. Kiwanis

35. Lions Club

36. Elks Club

37. Hunting licenses

38. Boating licenses

39. Voting registry

40. Court house

41. Bus stop

42. Malls

43. Banks

44. Job/workforce centers
45. VoTech Schools
46. Trade schools
47. Baby Announcements
48. Wedding announcements
49. promotion or job new hire announcements in newspapers
50. VA
51. Auto shop
52. Trade shows
53. Conventions
54. Concerts
55. Sporting events
56. Park
57. Seasonal sporting teams
58. Wal-Mart (like stores)
59. SAMS Club (like stores)
60. Hospitals
61. Everywhere customer transactions take-place
62. Video Stores
63. Friends
64. Newspaper features, write-ups, people spot lights, etc.
65. Church
66. Internet
67. Unit commanders, leaders, personnel
68. Recent enlistments
69. Doctor's offices
70. Driver's license office
71. Tag agency for car plates, registration
72. Family members
73. Friends
74. Friends network of people they know
75. Neighbors
76. Spouses
77. Spouses work associates, friends, their families
78. YMCA
79. Coffee houses
80. Camp Grounds
81. Factories
82. Armory

83. Library
84. Civic volunteering
85. Fleet
86. Exhibit areas
87. USAREC Rec.
88. 1-800-Go-Guard leads
89. NGB Leads
90. Airports – workers, travelers, checking-in, baggage claim, etc.
91. Casino
92. Business/Factory closing outplacement informational exposure
93. Car lots/finance department
94. Hiking/Camping/Rafting/Outside Venues
95. Forestry Agencies
96. Unemployment and Job Search firms and Agencies
97. Chamber of Commerce – Networking events, committees, trade shows, etc.
98. Chamber of Commerce in mid to large metros have YP (Young Professional) groups
99. All First Responders, are pre-vetted for you and if between 25-35 years of age great POCs to share how the Guard can accelerate their career success and value to their market place
100. Etc.

COI Market

1. Consider every option below as 24/7 TREs, where do all of these leads work/live from 11PM-7AM
2. Review all above TREs from each list for possible COI identification and cultivation ... then,
3. Identify local market professional development and lead referral networking groups you can join, attend, or affiliate into: a. BNI.com b. Business Referral breakfast clubs c. Rotary.org d. Chamber-of-Commerce business groups e. Lions/Elk/Moose etc. clubs f. Kiwanis.org g. CEOSpace.com
4. VA Rep.
5. VA Hospital waiting areas, administration, Doctors, etc.

6. Any community Hospital building *& id appropriate TRE areas …
7. New Enlistees
8. Police officers
9. Firemen/professionals
10. Bus drivers
11. Radio station managers/DJs
12. TV announcers/station managers
13. Newspaper managing editors, assignment editors, Publishers
14. Unit commanders, leaders, personnel, Armory contacts…AGGRESSIVELY work these contacts!
15. Jaycees
16. Rotary, Optimists, Kiwanis, Elks Lodge, American Legion, Fraternal Orgs (and like groups and their leaders individually…)
17. City leaders, City Councilors, administrators, etc.
18. Retired area military
19. Barber shop
20. Doctor's
21. Mailman
22. USAREC Rec.
23. All LOCAL/MUNICIPAL government employees (pre-vetted)
24. All COUNTY government employees (pre-vetted)
25. All STATE government employees (pre-vetted)
26. All FEDERAL government employees in your area (pre-vetted)
27. Government Job Search, Jobs Corp & Employment Services Agencies
28. Local COMMERCIAL Job Search & Employment Services Company or Franchise
29. Etc.

Stay Away From Market … while there may some exceptions, when Units have attrition problems, when you can't get someone through MEPS and need waivers on a regular basis, maybe that is a clue that your recruitment habits have taken you to the bottom of the barrel and these bottom feeders are not what makes for an intelligent ARMY…consider the above outlets for increased recruitment performance and you will find that these areas will become a memory in your professional recruitment selling days

1. Bars
2. Strip Clubs
3. Jail
4. Court house
5. Street corner/gutter/curb/highway under-pass
6. Bus Stations
7. Etc.

BONUS Lead Generator:

Present Guard Member (Male/Female as appropriate):

1. Identify a Guardsman by age that is an ideal profile soldier, do this for every age segmentation from 17 through 35 years of age (this would be 18 new or better COI working with you and for you to better matriculate leads for presentations),
2. Get with each one in your area and build a trusting relationship with them, then invite them to be your strategic COI and feed you leads from their centerof-influence …
3. Identify their list of friends, family members, work colleagues, customers, vendors they interact with at work or as a customer, the list of associates from their volunteer organization participations/involvements, etc.

COI & Ideal Recruitment Analyzer -

Start with an inverted "L-Grid" on a sheet of paper. Then for your geography identify the best COI by name across the top of the horizontal axis line of the grid. Then leave the outside of the vertical axis line space blank. Instead concentrate on the inside of the "L-Grid" and start by doing a complete brain dump of all of the information (personally and professionally) that you know about that specific COI that you have identified.

369

When you have transferred from your head to the sheet of paper (or computer flow sheet if you choose to automate the process) all of the information that you know on that COI specific name, then go back to your first entry (and continue this exercise for each subsequent entry).

Now on the outside of the vertical axis line associate an appropriate descriptor or character identifier for that entry. Now use this as a "TEMPLATE" for each of the TREs on this LEAD GENERATOR form (AND, you can use this to identify those profile traits of individuals that do not make it through MEPS or that fail-out of BASIC to become a guide post of what not to recruit!!!)

Chapter 68

Performance Driven Selling©
Work Product & Frequency
Accelerates Selling, Lessons
Learned from Model 5-1-2-1-2-X-5™
Formula

For the past thirty-years I have done this exercise within the pharmaceutical industry, transportation (automotive, motorcycle, car services), hospitality space (restaurants, hotels, resorts, airlines), construction and manufacturing, as well as the professional services industry (accounting, legal, consultants, contract trainers in the talent space, insurance, and real estate), and insurance and real estate. In 2000, one of America's largest selling organizations asked me to help them determine exactly how you could create an environment by which super star sales professionals could be developed, replicated and sustained.

How could this be?

The talent development comes second, the analysis of the professional also comes second, and the paths of execution are limitless. Every job, role, or position carries with it two essential variables. When you study the high performers in a role you want duplicated, these two variables will become very evident. They are:

1. **Work Product** – First, in order to identify what work products generate meaningful results associated with the selling life-cycle, you must be unbiased, objective, and candid, and gather massive analytics from only those that consistently exceed selling goals and mission.

2. **Frequency** – Second, identify what intervals these work products must be executed at. It is like identifying the rhythm and cadence that calibrates one to success and execute it, no matter how unexciting it may be.

Create a list of the activities or Work products that must be done. Let's consider yes or no to these Work Product activities. Would they help or hinder selling and closing rates?

1. Meeting *New People* that do not know you or that your offer exists, in an effort to generate new interest, followers, suspects, prospects and new clients/customers/enlistments/members/orders

2. Engage *COI or VIP* to you, your organization, or your deliverables in an effort to generate good-will, gain insights, invite lead referrals, etc

3. **Make Presentations (or informational engagements)** to existing clients (or suspect and prospect TREs) for new and more business and make presentations to new people for new sales

4. *Connect with Existing Clients or Co-Workers* for follow-up to your sales, to ensure product deliverable, gain personal leads from those you are serving, access and network their circles-of-influence

5. *Make Site Visits* to ensure what you are selling is being delivered, and to see about on-site new opportunities

Once you have performed the research and attained the analytics that reveal what the exact Work Product must be versus what others would like it to be, then it is time to determine the Frequency flow for each Work product. Once these two are married together, you can calibrate your efforts.

Example:

I have done this with a manufacturing firm by sitting down with the Founder and CEO that built a multi-million-dollar business. He was very clear at what must be done, when it should take place, and how often. When executed, ROI was amazing and conversely when ROI by a sales professional was not obtained, the reverse analysis was staggering clear. If you don't do the Work Product with the associated Frequency, you will fail... every time.

25 New Daily Contacts – Reached Daily
10 COI/VIP Contacts Weekly
2 Appointments/Presentations Weekly
10 eDM Direct Connections Daily
2 eMedia Kit/eProposals Sent Weekly

The presentation of this formula for the National Guard has become bastardized over the years, as those training are further removed from ever having been a sustained rock star of success and further away from why this formula was originally created.

With the individual State National Guard Recruiters and their sales management teams, if a Recruiter calibrates their behaviors off of this formula, then the math clearly shows sales success can be obtained within nine-months of every twelve-month period.

5 New Contacts Daily
1 COI/VIP Visit Per Week
2 Appointments Per Week
1 School Visit Per Week
2 Soldier Contacts Per Day
X Social Media Posts/Likes/Links/ Leverage/ Follow Daily
5 Inactive Activations Weekly

And, then as markets evolve, so too does your model of Work Product and Frequency. More than a decade ago I evolved this original 2000 Model with another Work product variable – Now it is 5-1-2-1-2-X with the X representing Internet/Social Media and daily connectivity to your market, contacts, clients.

It is human behavior to resist anything one fears will be restrictive or punishing in nature. If someone is introduced to this strategic concept as a penalty for not making their sales goals, they will reject it. If you present this to your sales team, avoid positioning it as punishment.

Thirty-years of research within www.ProfessionalPerformanceMagazine.com of super stars across the globe, industry, clearly shows that to achieve mediocrity, very little has to be done today. To obtain greatness, study those that are great (health, fitness, financial, business, medicine, art. music, entertainment, athletics, etc.) and you will see the analytics of their Work Product and the degree of Frequency that they commit to and execute.

Chapter 69

**Performance Driven Selling©
Sales Business Plans (SBP):
Designing & Implementing
Your Annual SBP for Daily ROI**

Amazing how we plan to succeed at the little things in life, yet we fail to plan to succeed for the big things. Consider:

1. Do you use a grocery list when you go to the grocery store?

2. For the Holidays, if you are shopping for several people do you have a plan, a check-list, items saved in your electronic devices?

3. If you go on a major vacation, would you do research, get options and pricing, and look at the data before making your final decisions?

4. If you were moving, would you research your options, the communities, the living spaces and calibrate that with your finances and your short or long-term needs? Would you have anything written down?

For most people the response to these types of questions is a resounding "yes!"

Yet, I find that a disproportionate number of sales professionals have no executable selling plan and wonder why they seldom exceed their selling goals, and in some cases, do not even make their sales goals.

If you were asked right now to go to your computer and hit print on your *Annual Sales Plan (SBP)*, what would you be able to produce? My experience over several decades working with everyone from the Fortune 500 to solo entrepreneur, is that the answer is often nothing or nothing meaningful, absent of measurable KPIs.

There are a lot of analytics that can be involved in designing and implementing your SBP and your unique market challenges and deliverables will dictate the nuances necessary for a sound SBP. Let's discuss a universal approach to get you and your sales management mindset calibrated for success.

Start by getting (in writing) what your organization's minimum expectations are of you as the sales representative (regardless of your working title) to the organization. If analytics are available, consider this data against what the historical data reveals for past occupants to your position. Then benchmark this annual accomplishment off of this year's current #1 selling professional. This data can be used as reference off of the following SBP work product; as you may find that the best-selling member to your organization has actually been under-performing.

In designing your *Annual Sales Business Plan (SBP),* consider the following template as a flow. Put your cursor at the end of each section prompt and if relevant start answering. If you can answer in a sentence, perfect, and if it takes 30-pages, that is also perfect. As you work this SBP template, you will begin to see what sections are missing for your industry and market. Add them and delete any non-relevant sections. The data this exercise produces will become the selling market intelligence that will guide you in your annual, quarterly, monthly and weekly action plans. This will allow you to budget time, resources, manpower, finances, etc. accordingly so you win every day and every month throughout the entire year.

The analytics of where your market is, where your competition wars against you, and where the emerging markets will be, all plays into an SBP. NO other strategic tool has the ROI of an SBP.

In one twelve-month period, the ARMY National Guard and the Sales Recruiters in the field in six states used this model along with other Performance Driven Selling programs we delivered. All six States made their sales Mission, while no other states succeeded. I have these templates for all of our clients from professional services industry to manufacturing to finance to distribution firms.

Some variables for inclusion in your SBP could be:

1. Detail out the Avatar to your organization including where and how to connect with them, where and when that Avatar is available to you and what their buying needs and cycles are.
2. Benchmark the last 36-months of where, when and who bought your offer
3. Identify the primary markets for your Avatar and when, where, how to engage them
4. Identify the secondary markets for your Avatar and when, where, how to engage them
5. Identify the tertiary markets for your Avatar and when, where, how to engage them
6. Identify what percentage of the market you get presently versus the competition, and use reverse analysis for the past 36-months. Evaluate why you get that percentage and why the competition gets their percentage

7. Now, transition to market potential or market abundance mentality and explore the totality of suspects in your market that are not buying you nor anyone and that you could go after. Where, when and how?
8. Explore why you are losing sales and how you can regain that %
9. Explore why others are losing sales and how you can gain their %
10. How do you address your COI placement and touch-points?
11. How do you address special events, holidays, situational market and avatar needs?

To further accelerate your strategic selling abilities consider getting copies of SBPs from:

1. Your organization archives
2. Trade Associations
3. Professional selling journals, magazines, periodicals, bloggers
4. On-line search engine platforms (google searches) and search for down loads
5. Inquire with colleagues into their professional selling capacities, if they have one or of their organization has one, get copies for thought patterns that can be replicated
6. Do you have competition and if so do they have strategic selling plans or annual SBPs and can you get a copy to see how the KPIs are built off of their game plans

A great SBP should allow you to benchmark your daily, weekly and monthly activities for accountability. Quarterly check-ups with your SBP is a great self-accountability tool. All consistent winning organizations actually plan to succeed at the little things and the big things. Their SBP drives their daily KPIs to ensure that the trajectory one is on, leads to a win in the end.

Chapter 70

Performance Driven Selling©
What Does RIGHT Look Like?

When you evaluate the *actions, behaviors* and *characteristics* (ABCs) of the super achievers in any vocation, capacity or position, you begin to recognize what right looks like. Only when you have objective, reality-based analytics, you can benchmark excellence from rhetoric and calibrate every second of the day for excellence.

Unfortunately in far too many industries, I've seen "the blind leading the blind." There are quantifiably inept individuals being placed into positions to train, influence and make policy over what professional selling individuals are supposed to execute.

So, what does right look like? Consider:

1. **Start With The End In Mind** – Does your organization already has a matrix by which everyone is evaluated and from which one person rises to the top award, citation, medal, accommodation (Chairman's Award, President's Cup, Directors Award, Million-Dollar-Roundtable, Etc.)? Then evaluate the ABCs of that person and determine how you do the same as a minimum.

2. **Certification** – If your position had a certification process, would you be able to attain it and maintain it daily? Are you or would you be in compliance with the

qualifications? Typically, in any legitimate trade there are certifications and or levels of growth that carry higher and higher levels of validation. Think about what an Engineer, Lawyer, CP has to accomplish to gain their initial credentials and then what must they do as a minimum annually to maintain their license to practice? As a selling professional how would you structure your professionalism?

3. **Work Product & Frequency** – Do you really know what work products must be done for minimum effectiveness and maximum performance success? Then once those are quantifiable, have you done the math to determine the frequency of each work product?

4. **Shadow Time** – Do you get the opportunity to network, intern, serve as an apprentice or shadow fellow great achievers to learn from them and develop mental models of excellence to calibrate your ABC off of?

5. **Training Time** – Do you have a clear set of sequential, chronological talent development pathways for continuous learning and improvement in your craft? Is this set to a calendar so you know, regardless of what your employer provides, what you must do annually to maintain viability?

6. **Funnel Time** – Do you an understanding of every aspect before, within and after the selling funnel or selling pipeline and what strategically one must do to have fluid constructive activities and productive applications for lead flow, market awareness and client/sale cultivation?

7. **Product Knowledge Time** – Do you have a working understanding of the breath of deliverables you have to offer and how this influences your ability to see the market potentials?

8. **Administrative Time** – Do you understand and possess the most effective understanding of the business-of-the-business side of what you do? Do you have a list of KPI (Key Performance Indicators) from the proven achiever in your space regarding what must be done, when it must be done, what hurdles that could derail your success, and have predetermined workarounds to them when they rise?

9. **Entrepreneurial Time** – Are you a practitioner of your business or do you possess the ability to be the innovator to the business?

10. **Synergistic Time** – Do you understand how everything that you do has interconnectivity? Do you leverage what you do and who you know for accelerated growth and pure ROI?

So, what does right look like for you? Evaluate what right looked like for anyone historically within your organization, vocation or industry and you will have a clear road map.

Chapter 71

Performance Driven Selling© Rule 5@5™ is the Ultimate Self-Accountability Assessment for Closing More Sales!

Whether you have an automated system to assist you or you're old school and you just write this down on a piece-of-paper or whiteboard, the concept is golden for personal self-accountability and significantly increased, focused mental effort in closing more sales.

Every Friday by 5PM you identify the top/best 5 contacts, prospects, avatars/leads/clients that you are working towards your next sale/recruitment/enlistment and you identify exactly what must be done next to move them forward through your sales pipeline/funnel to closure – hence 5@5.

You could even have categories of 5@5 …

1. Top potential sales for my organization over-all
2. Top potential sales by product or brand category
3. Top potential sales by SKU/item/deliverable
4. Top potential sales by any other way you do business
a. Industry
b. Geography
c. Sales representative
d. Etc.

Without a tool as simple as this you can get buried with data and far too many distracting analytics. If you have a sales boss or you are a sales leader, this is a powerful way to end each week by zeroing in your efforts on a quantifiable target list of 5@5 and engaging up or down for insights for next best course of engagement actions.

This 5@5 approach also allows you to reflect on your entire selling efforts for what is working and what is not working. For example, if you are deploying Rule 1-52-X every Monday, this becomes a way to hold yourself accountable at the end of the week.

You can personalize this even further by placing a personal calendar reminder into your database, CRM or cell phone calendar system as a perpetual reoccurring Friday alarm reminder. Log it in at "3:17PM – Review 5@5" as the likelihood of you ever needing to log a reminder, event, meeting, call, etc. at that awkward time is low to never, so it is always there a few hours before the end of the day on Friday as a business development reminder … Rule 5@5 is just simple and powerful at yielding ROI!

ABOUT THE AUTHOR

Dr. Jeffrey Magee

PhD, CBE, CSP, CMC, PDM

… has been called one of today's leading **"Leadership & Marketing Strategists."** Today, under JeffreyMagee, LLC, Magee works with C-Suite, Business Owners & Leaders, Military Generals, Entrepreneurial Unicorns, CEO2CEO Peer Groups & YPO leaders across the globe.

Jeff is the Author of more than 20 books, translated into 21-languages, three college graduate management text books, four best sellers, the Publisher of *PERFORMANCE/P360 Magazine* (www.ProfessionalPerformanceMagazine.com), former Co-Host of the national business entrepreneur program on Catalyst Business Radio (http://www.catalystbusinessradio.com/index.php), and a Human Capital Developer for more than twenty years with www.JeffreyMagee.com.

Professional Credentials:

Magee is committed to professional excellence for you his client and his on-going certification credentials are significant. Along with advanced degrees, he is a *Certified Board Executive (CBE), Certified Speaking Professional (CSP), a Certified Management Consultant (CMC),* and a *Certified Professional Direct Marketer (PDM).*

Experience:

The *"Thought Leader's Leader"* ... Dr. Jeffrey Magee brings over three decades of Executive, Corporate and Talent Development expertise, working in both the start-up to mature-growth market business sector and with differing State National Guard Adjutant Generals across America. Jeff has and does maintain long term clients working with Association and Organizations at the Board level and across the C-Suite. Beyond this, the importance of working with an organizations entire Human Capital platform from on-boarding, integration, and sustained engagement is critical for an organization's health blue-print. Jeff works with organizations (profit and not-for-profit, private and public sector) in the multi-million-dollar earnings market through to major billion-dollar earning market leaders.

Unlike most consultants that bring only "book-expertise" to a situation or client, Magee brings the battle tested talent of having actually done what we talk's and consults about – from wins to failures!

For more than three-decades his ideas and business operating models have disrupted conventional wisdom within **SHRM**/Society for Human Resource Management (https://www.shrm.org/), *ASTD/**ATD**/Association for Talent Development* (https://www.td.org/), **YPO**/*Young Presidents' Organization* (https://www.ypo.org/about-ypo/), VISTAGE CEO leaders, and the **NSA**/*National Speakers Association* (https://www.nsaspeaker.org/) ...

Recognitions:

He has been recognized as one of the **"Ten Outstanding Young Americans"** (TOYA) by the U.S. Junior Chamber of Commerce, and twice selected to represent the United States at the World Congress as a Leadership Speaker (Cannes, France and Vienna, Austria). A three-term President of the Oklahoma Speakers Association and twice awarded their Professional

Speaker Member of the Year, today, the Chapter's outstanding member of the year is awarded the *"Jeff Magee Member of the Year Award."* Jeff served for four years as an appointed Civil Service Commissioner (Judge) for the City/County of Tulsa Oklahoma, before relocating to Montana in 2010.

Work History/Today:

Understanding the reality of hard work ethics and drive from an early age, raised on a farm, Jeff started his first business at age 15 and sold it before going to college. By age 24, he was recognized by American Home Products a Fortune 100 company as its top salesman in the nation, while at the same time becoming the youngest certified sales instructor globally for the **Dale Carnegie Sales Course**. After experiencing downsizing in 1987, he went on to work as a sales associate for the nation's largest educational and youth advertising/marketing firm, Target Marketing, and was promoted to Vice President of Sales and Chief Operating Officer within two years.

Today, Magee is the author of the nationally syndicated "LEADERSHIP MASTERY: Managerial-Leadership" column targeted towards business owners, leaders and the C-Suite that you may have seen in your local business newspaper or on-line and the nationally syndicated "SALES MASTERY: Performance Driven Selling" column. And serves as the publisher of *Professional Performance Magazine/PERFORMANCE360 (www.ProfessionalPerformanceMagazine.com)* – a Quarterly success achievement publication with editorial contributions for the World's leading personalities.

Jeff is the author of more than 20 leadership, performance, and sells books that have been transcribed into multiple languages including four best-sellers. In fact, his text, *Yield Management* has been a #1 selling graduate management school textbook with *CRC Press*, while *The Sales Training Handbook* by *McGraw-Hill* was an instant best seller and has been transcribed into more than 20 languages. While his newest books *it!* and *Your Trajectory Code* released January 2015 by *John Wiley, the world's largest trade book publisher*, are best-sellers. *The Managerial-Leadership Bible, Revised Edition* his fourth college text book released in 2016 by PEARSON EDUCATION, the world's largest academic text book publisher is changing how people look at human capital development and engagement!

His signature managerial-leadership engagement development series *THE LEADERSHIP ACADEMY OF EXCELLENCE®,* a twelve-month accredited talent development program, is utilized by many of the Fortune 100 firms, the ARMY National Guard, Federal Reserve, Farm Credit Banks, as well as Entrepreneurial business owners today at the C-Suite level and as an interactive engaged managerial-leadership effectiveness series with senior leaders. This program has been recognized as one of the leading Executive Development Programs (EDP), Leadership Development Programs (LDP), and Managerial Development Programs (MDP) today. Understanding human capital performance and talent development, Jeff has a unique lens for revenue generation in everything he does and this is enhanced with his extensive sales training and coaching options for B2B and B2C utilization.

Magee was commissioned to design, train, and present a new series of national leadership and sales recruitment programs for more than the 3,500 professional sales recruiters and sales managers with the **U.S. Army National Guard.** For this he has subsequently received numerous prestigious **Commander's Coin of Excellence.** He also been invited to keynote at many major associations in America and at **West Point Military Academy** on leadership. In, 2010 while merging his business JEFF MAGEE INTERNATIONAL (Tulsa, OK) of 20 years with Western CPE (Bozeman, MT), managing and developing a staff of more than 140 professionals, he steered a business from near financial collapse to significant profitability in a billion-dollar market segmentation – in six accelerated months. While expanding market opportunities, deliverables, and creating new revenue streams, Magee also created more than 2,000-hours of accredited CPE human capital professional development and leadership courseware.

Simultaneously, Magee was recognized as **The U.S. Small Business Commerce Association (SBCA)** 2010 Best of Business Award in the Lecture bureau category. The SBCA Best of Business Award Program recognizes the best of small businesses throughout the country. Using consumer feedback and other research, the SBCA identifies companies that we believe have demonstrated what makes small businesses a vital part of the American economy. The

selection committee chooses the award winners from nominees based off information taken from monthly surveys administered by the SBCA, a review of consumer rankings, and other consumer reports. Award winners are a valuable asset to their community and exemplify what makes small businesses great.

In 2011, Magee un-merged from Western CPE to continue with his own firm *JeffreyMagee.com* (*Leadership Training & Technology/What You Need to Succeed!*), and has been a regular content provider to AICPA, Western CPE, Boomer Consulting, iShade, CPELink, and many of the Fortune 500 Firms and Government Agencies, as well as appearing regularly at major conventions and conferences around the World. Twice invited to Keynote at the World Congress (Cannes, France and Vienna, Austria), Jeff is known to many as the *"thought leaders, thought leader"*!

With more than 2,000 hours of accredited CPE/CLE courseware and consulting deliverables for CPAs, EAs and Attorney's, Jeff has worked with and trained some of America's leading Subject-Matter-Experts (SMEs) within America's top consulting, accounting and legal organizations!

Over the past three decades leading training and development organizations such as Fred Pryor Seminars, SkillPath Seminars, CareerTrack Seminars, American Management Association, the Conference Board, AICPA, and Fortune 100 training enterprises have contracted with Magee to design courseware for them and provide train-the-trainer programs to equip others with his technologies to lead countless others to performance excellence around the World.

SELLING Centric:

Today, the bedrock of his sales mastery professional development programs are the ***SALES MASTERY: Performance Driven Selling™/1.0/2.0/3/0/4.0*** Series (www.JeffreyMagee.com), each one highly tailored to the clients' needs and with massive sustainment resources built in for greater ROI for the client!

Jeff has uncovered quantifiable models for selling success that have been replicated across industries with proven, vetted results. He has the ***Systems, Processes and Procedures*** that can take a new sales professional to success in a very short cycle and can accelerate veteran sales professionals to amazing sustained achievement levels. From Fortune 500 Firms to mid-cap businesses, all of benefited greatly from his course-ware, content and deliverables.

Along with his on-site in-house professional development KEYNOTES and engaged TRAINING PROGRAMS, he regularly offers the 2-day ***SALES MASTERY: Performance Driven Selling Bootcamp™/1.0 – Fundamentals to Selling Success***, go to www.JeffreyMagee.com/events as an open-enrollment public event, to learn more about that 2-day experience, times and location.

Magee is the writer of ***SALES MASTERY: Performance Driven Selling™*** and ***SALES MASTERY: Performance Driven Recruitment Selling™*** a weekly syndicated article series on selling that appears nationally in newspapers, on-line as a newsletter and blog with more than 100 strategic and tactical selling articles in this category alone.

Jeff is the author of the McGraw-Hill best-selling institutional and collegiate text book, *THE SALES TRAINING HANDBOOK©* with 52-weekly selling self mini-seminars for business owners, sales managers and sales trainers to easily use with their teams weekly. This book has been translated into 21-languages, for readership application across the Globe. Other selling specific centric works by Magee include the wildly successful book *it! How To Find It, Get It, Keep It & Grow IT©*, a book of more than 400 immediate applicable selling strategies and techniques address the 360-degrees of selling, the *it! How To Find It, Get It, Keep It & Grow IT©* CD Series of the same name with more than 100 power Podcasts, and his best-selling DVD Series *Performance Driven Selling©™*!

His newest book, *SALES MASTERY: Performance Driven Selling - 101 Immediate Strategies & Techniques for Massive Sustained Return On Investment©* takes the discussion of professional selling to new heights.

With this new publication, Jeff has also released a special edition, *SALES MASTERY: Performance Driven Selling for the MILITARY RECRUITER - 101 Immediate Strategies & Techniques for Massive Enlistment Success!©* These *Systems, Process and Procedures* in one year alone were credited by six out of the only seven States of the United States National Guard Recruiting Command in America to make Mission – and one State went from #50 to #2 in 18-months using his programming!

Jeff has also designed an extensive self-paced 25-module *SALES MASTERY: Performance Driven Selling™* on-line Learning Management System, with fully integrated training webinars, mini manuals, podcasts, eBooks, developmental blogs, acceleration worksheets, audio and DVD learning programs, digital copies of PERFORMANCE MAGAZINE and more for client use – whether you are new to selling, want to brush-up on professional selling or you are a seasoned veteran selling professionals.

For more than two-decades as a performance psychologist, Jeff has interviewed, coached and studied the top achieving sales professionals within his Fortune 100 clients and the United States National Guard Recruiters to learn and gather the analytics to very specific and quantifiable KPIs to achieving and exceeding sales campaign goals. To add to the science and art of peak performance, Jeff has for more than 20-years served as the Publisher to ***Performance Magazine*™**, whereby the world's most successful individuals share their strategies, techniques, secrets and insights to accelerated success. Legends of the selling and human improvement space have written for Jeff and have shared stages with one another – *Zig Ziglar, Tom Hopkins, Mark Victor Hansen, Jack Canfield, Sharon Lechter, Tony Robbins, Les Brown, Harvey MacKay, Stephen Covey* and many more - https://www.professionalperformancemagazine.com/

The *London Business Gazette* has hailed Jeff as "*An American Business Guru.*" **Recipient of the prestigious United States Junior Chamber of Commerce's "Ten Outstanding Young Americans" (TOYA) Award, former President** George Bush and the U.S. Army National Guard recognized him with the high honor of the **"Total Team Victory & Freedom Award."** However, more important than Magee's credentials and accomplishments, he is market proven and here today to serve you.

TO BOOK JEFF - Jeff can be scheduled for your next Conference, Convention, Retreat, and Consulting or for an On-Site high impact results driven development program by contacting: Jeffrey@JeffreyMagee.com.
www.JeffreyMagee.com